HAL•LEONARD

BASS PLAY·ALONG™

VOL. 51

CONTENTS

Cover photo: Ken Settle

ISBN 978-1-4950-2260-9

HAL•LEONARD®
CORPORATION

7777 W. BLUEMOUND RD. P.O. BOX 13819 MILWAUKEE, WI 53213

In Australia Contact:
Hal Leonard Australia Pty. Ltd.
4 Lentara Court
Cheltenham, Victoria, 3192 Australia
Email: ausadmin@halleonard.com.au

Visit Hal Leonard Online at
www.halleonard.com

Couldn't Stand the Weather

Written by Stevie Ray Vaughan

Tune down 1/2 step:
(low to high) E♭-A♭-D♭-G♭

Intro
Free time

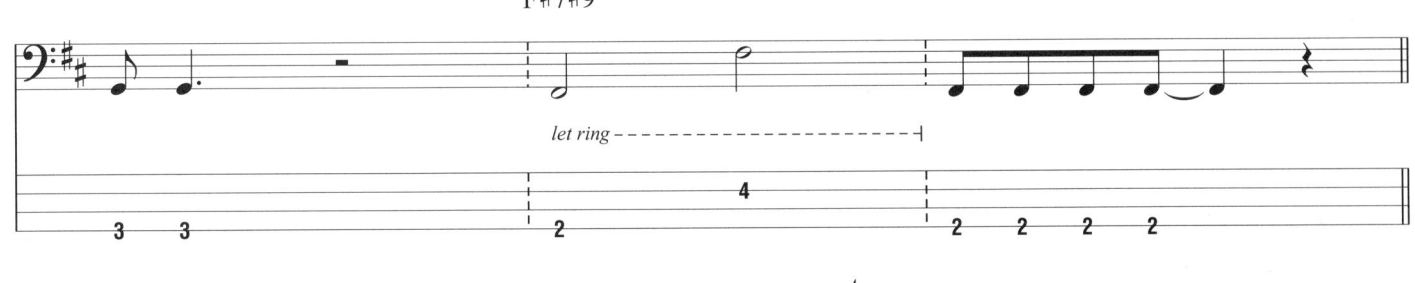

D7#9   G   D7#9

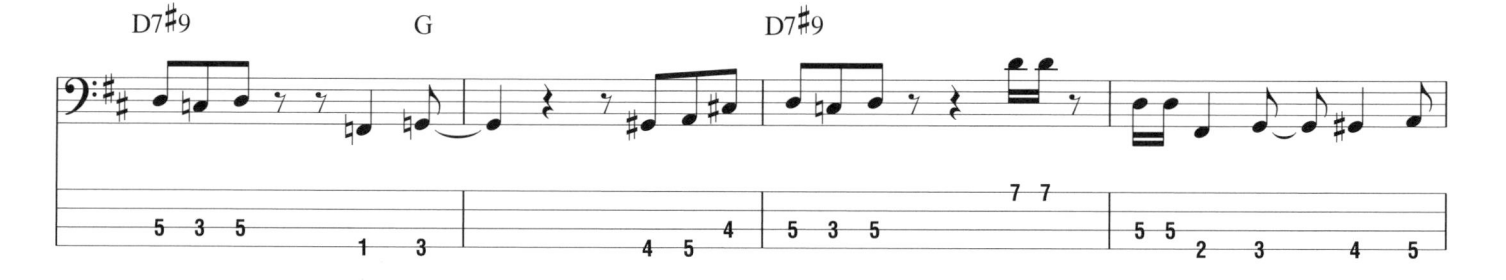

                 G   D7#9

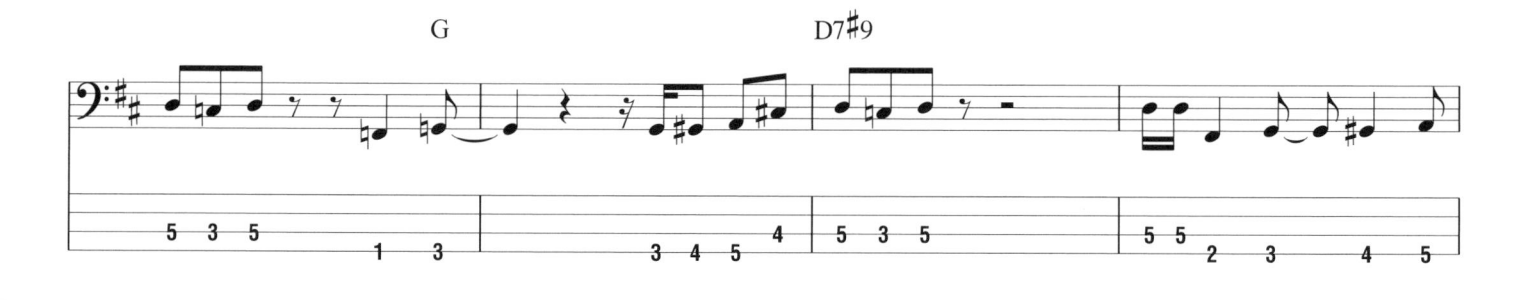

                 G   D7#9

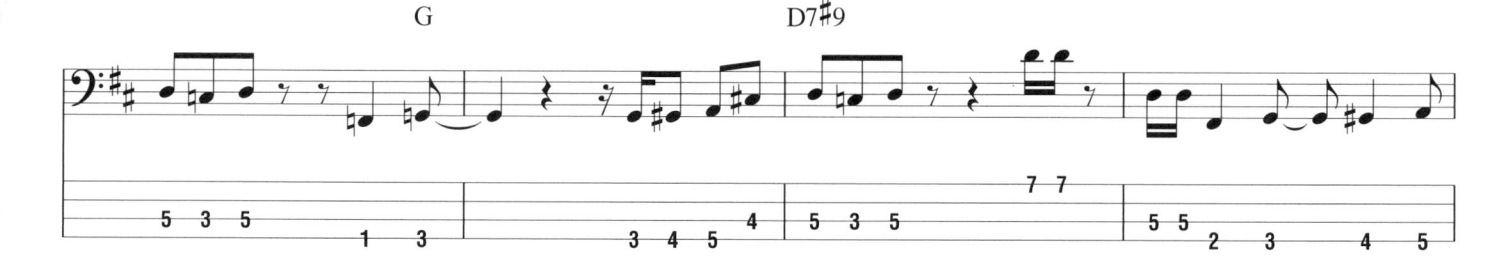

                 G   D7#9

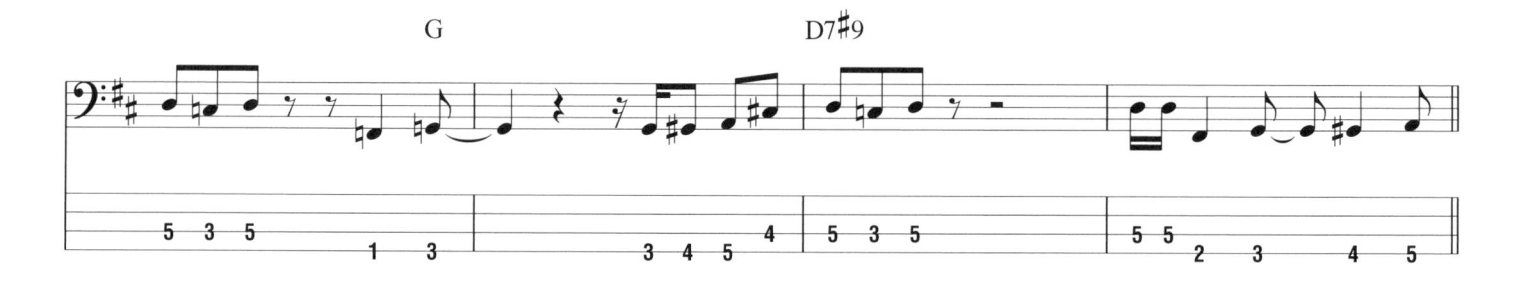

Verse

D7#9

1. Com-in' through ___ this a bus-'ness of life, ___

en - tan-gled in yel - low and cries _____ all his tears.

Bm

Chang-es come _ be - fore we can go. _____

A9

Learn to see them be - fore _____ we're too old. _____

G9

Don't just take me for try'n' to be heav - y.

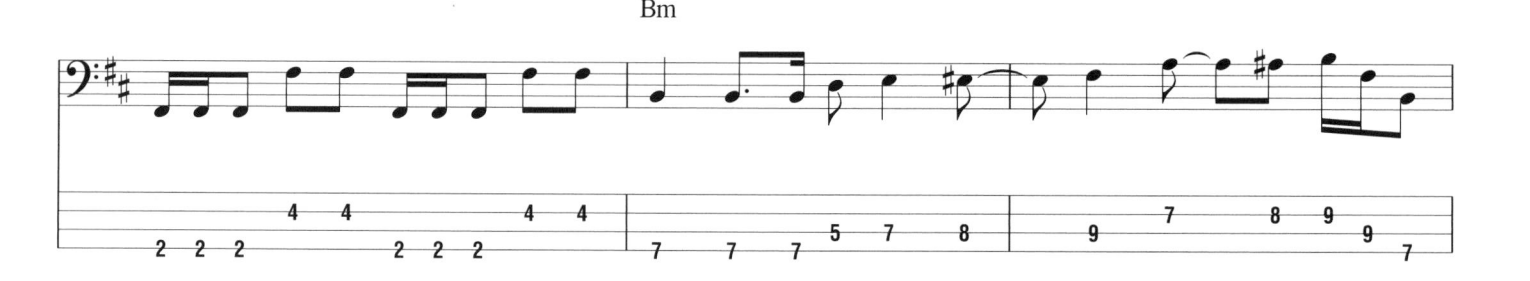

Pride and Joy

Written by Stevie Ray Vaughan

Tune down 1/2 step:
(low to high) E♭-A♭-D♭-G♭

Intro

Moderate Blues ♩ = 126 (♫ = ♩♪ triplet)

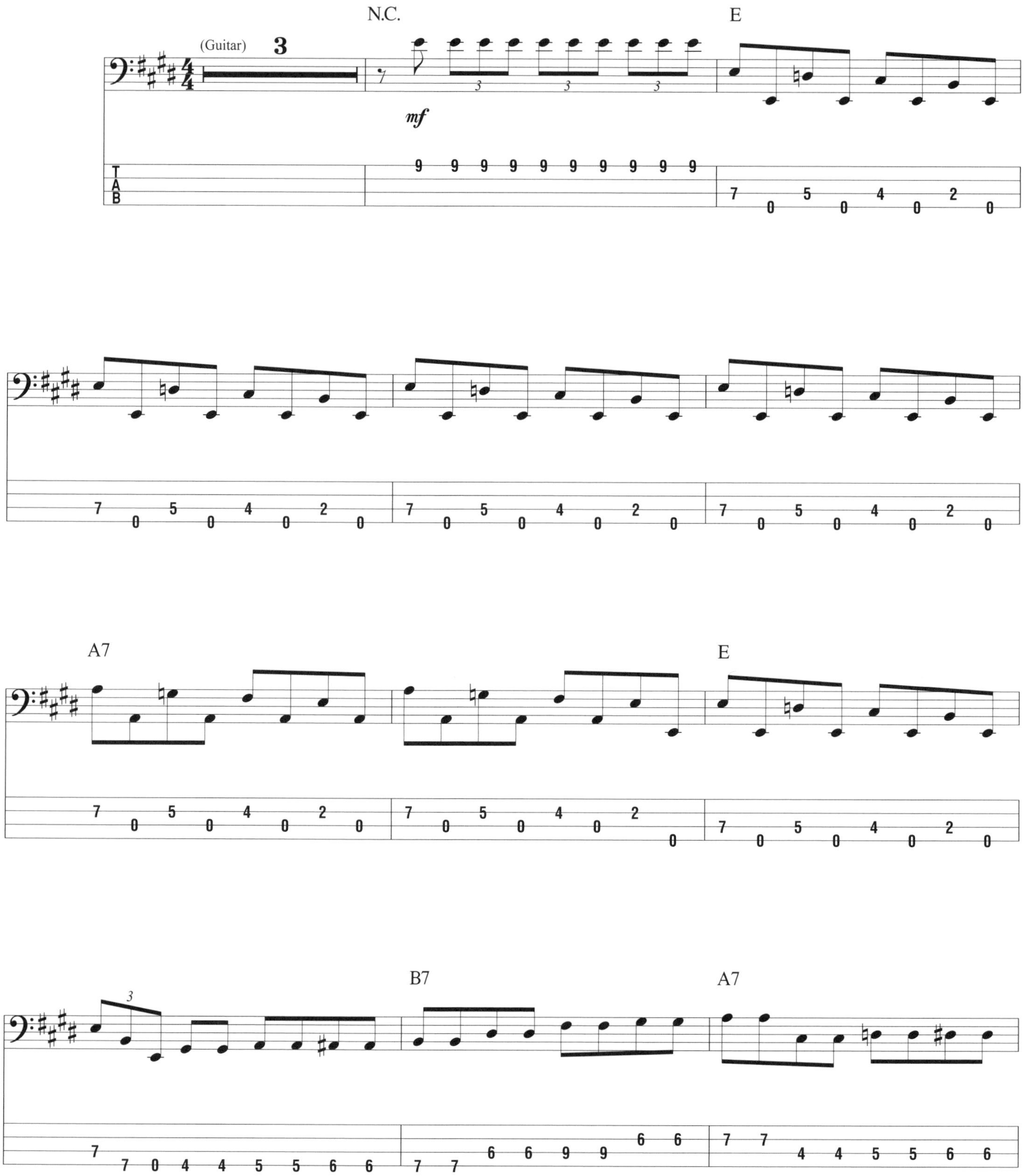

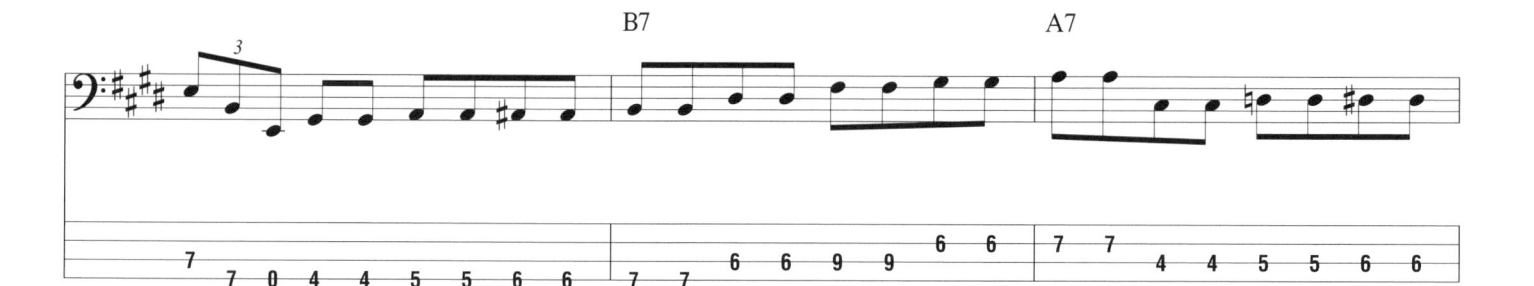

E
B7
3. Yeah, I
Verse
E N.C.
E N.C.
E N.C.
love my la - dy to be long and lean.
You mess with her, you'll see a
E
A7
man get - tin' mean. She('s) my sweet lit - tle thang,
she('s) my
E
B7
pride and joy.
She('s) my sweet lit - tle ba - by, I'm

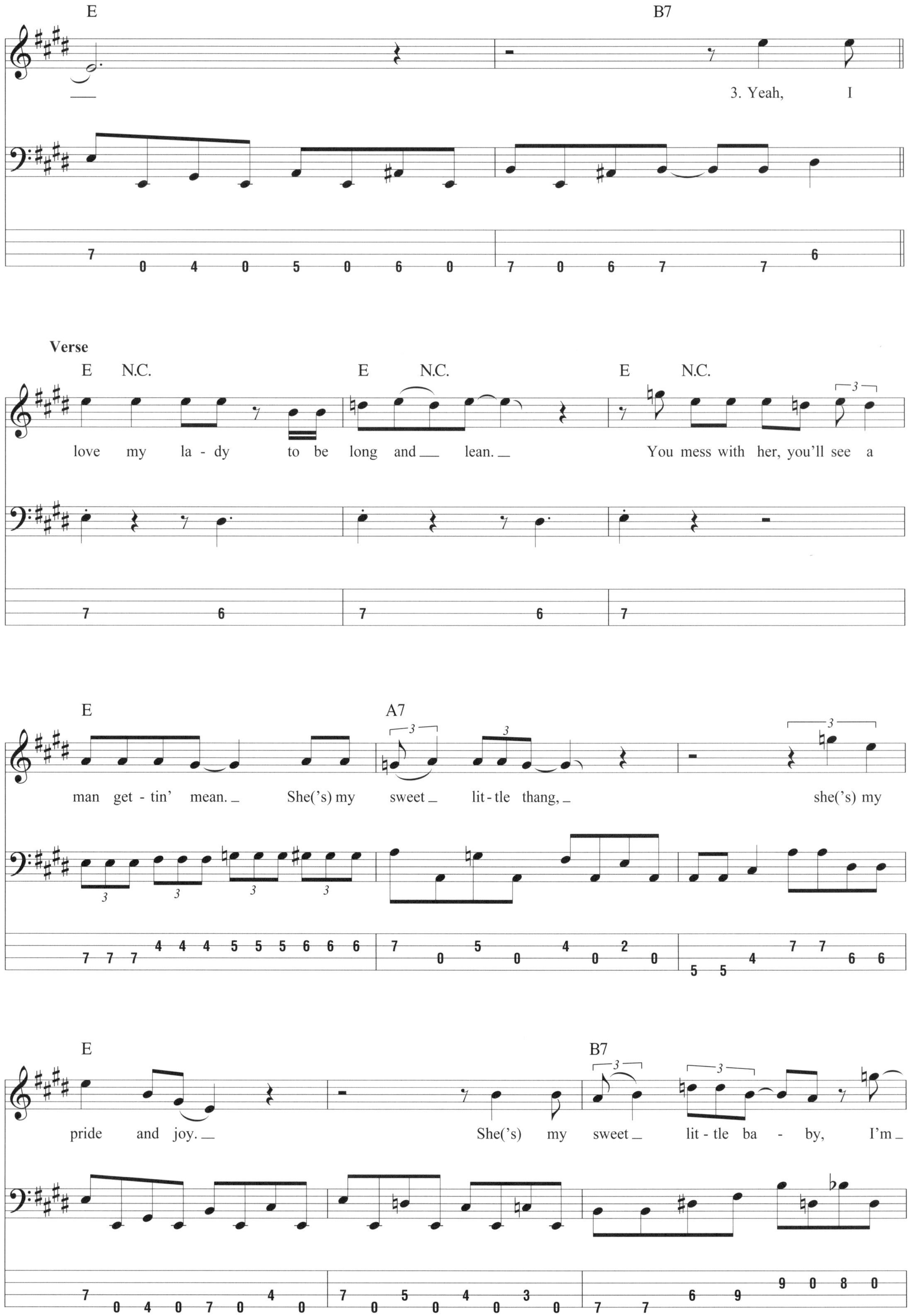

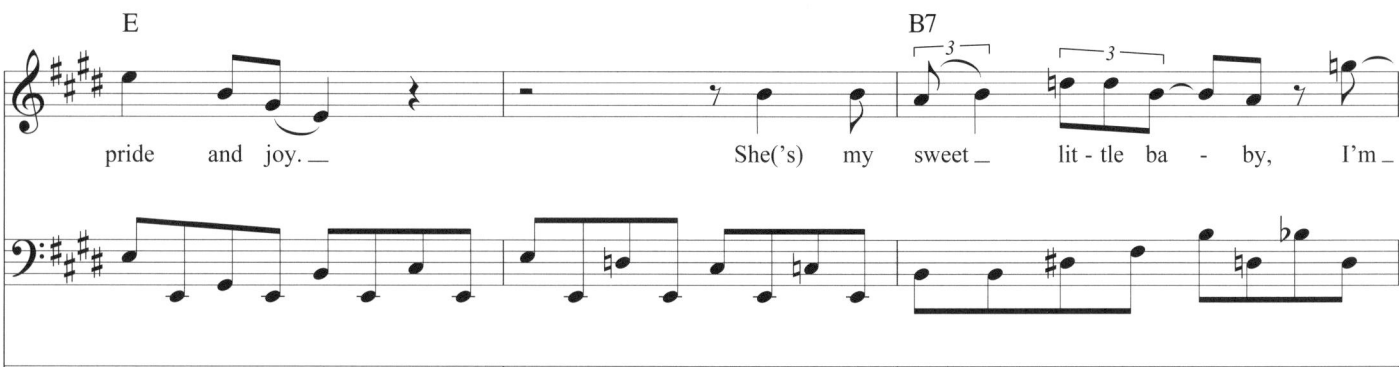

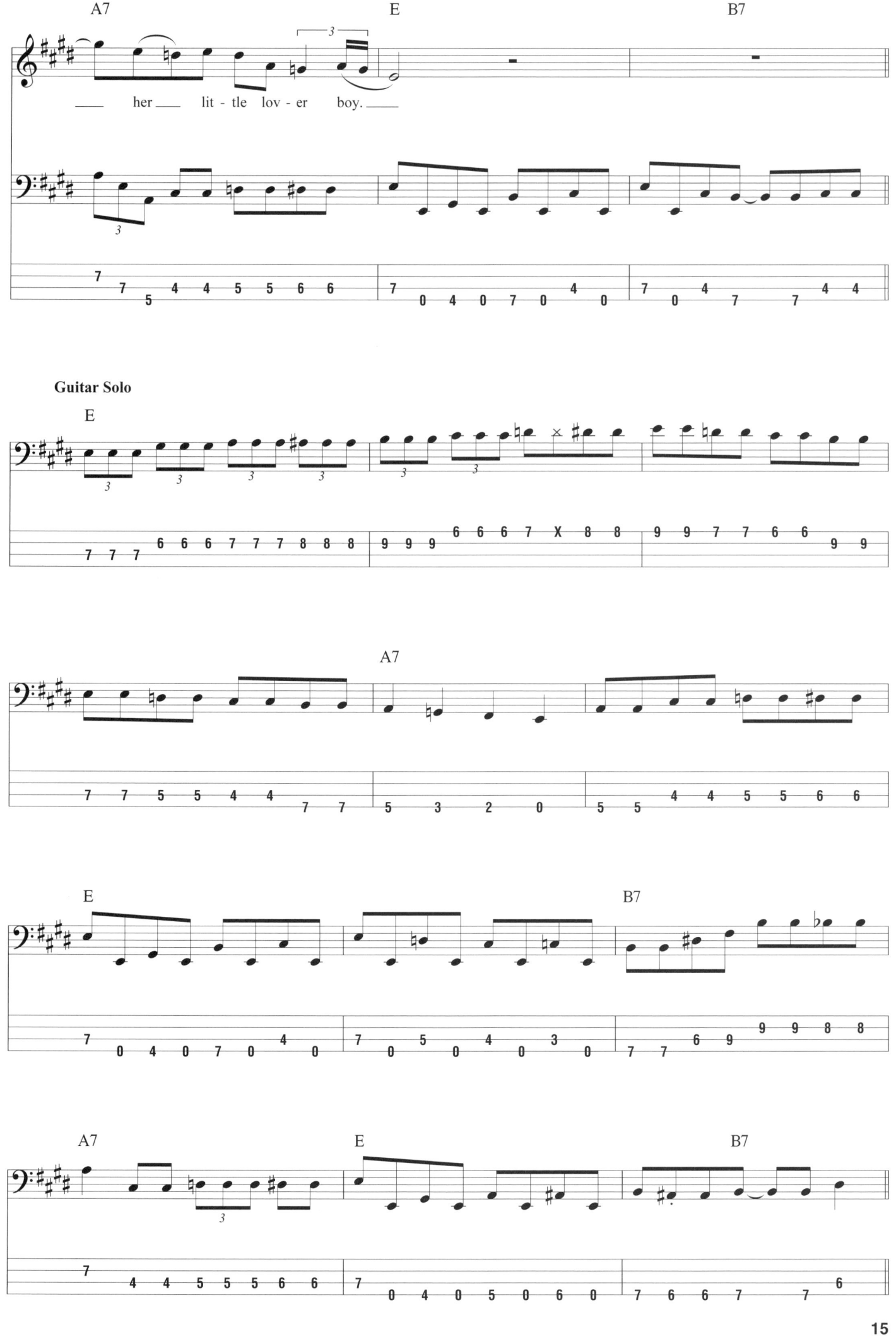

Guitar Solo

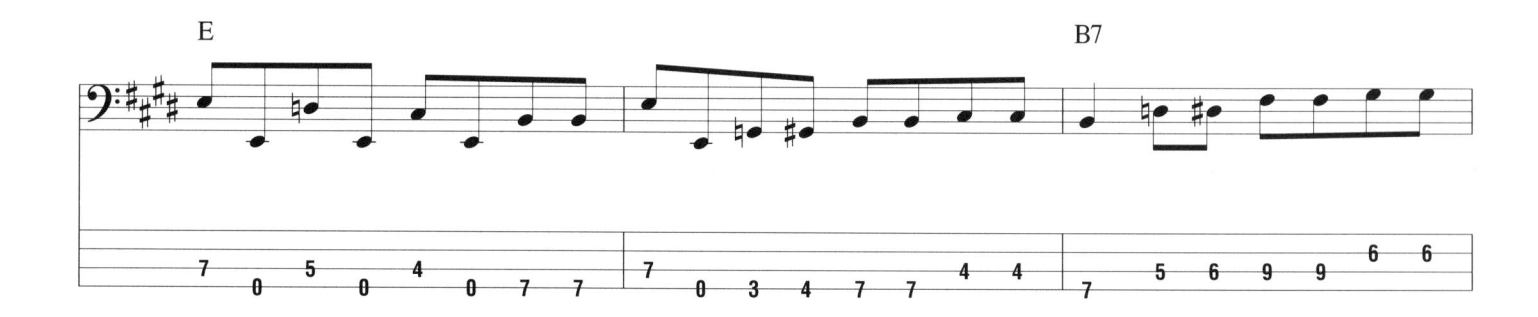

4. Well,   I

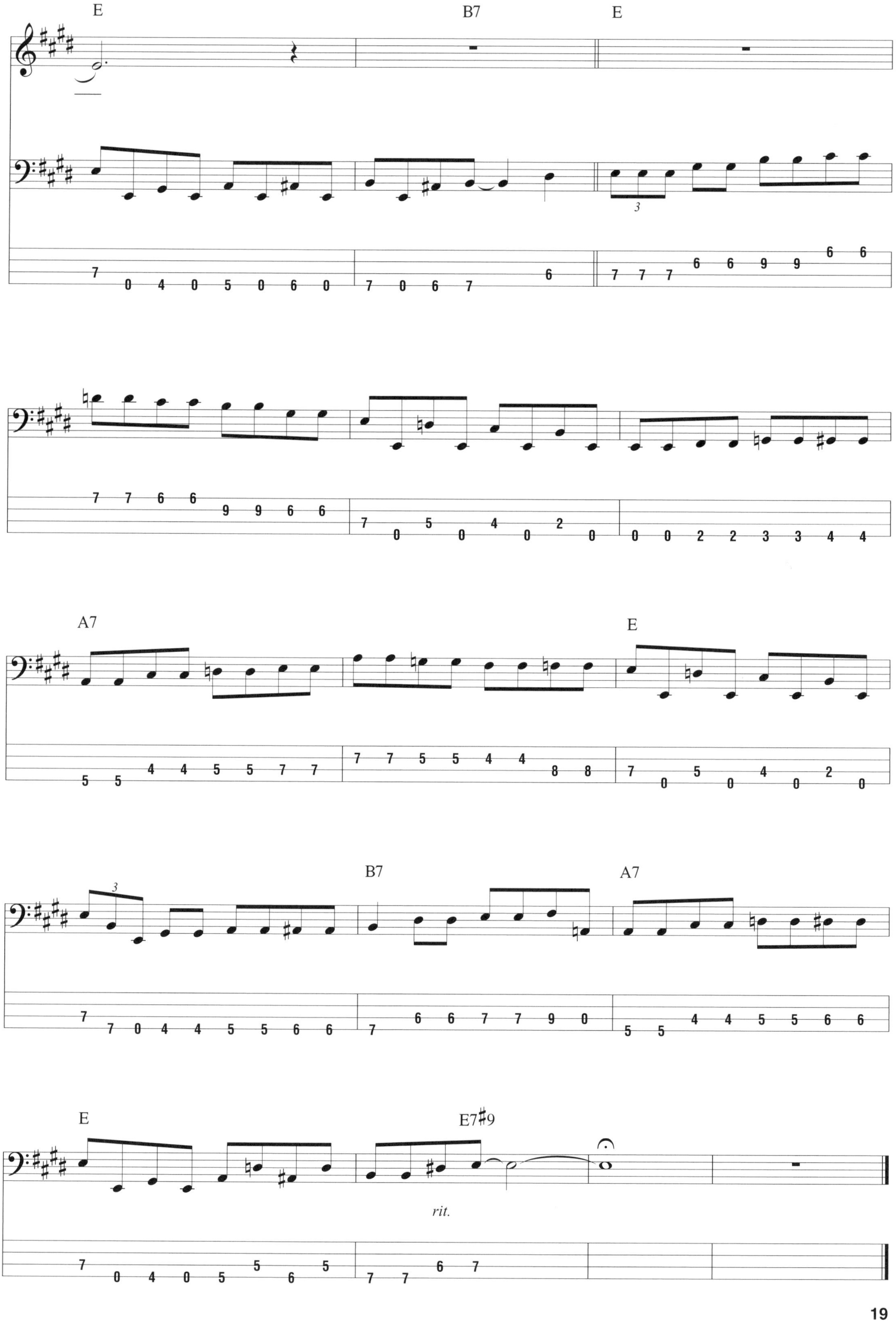

Crossfire

Words and Music by Bill Carter, Ruth Ellsworth, Reese Wynans, Tommy Shannon and Chris Layton

fire?

I am strand - ed, _____

To Coda ⊕

caught in the cross - fire.

Bridge

G   A   G

I need some   kind of kind - ness, ___   some kind of sym-pa - thy. __

Chorus

A   E7

___ Oh,   no,   we're strand - ed, _____   caught in the cross -

-fire.

Guitar Solo

E7

Play 8 times

G

A

G

A

2nd time, D.S. al Coda

E7

Coda

We got strand - ed, _____

Outro-Guitar Solo

caught in the cross - fire.

Strand-ed, _____ caught in ___ the cross - fire.

Help me!

E7

Play 7 times

N.C.   E7

Additional Lyrics

3. Save the strong, lose the weak,
   Never turnin' the other cheek.
   Trust nobody, don't be no fool.
   Whatever happened to the golden rule?
   We got stranded,...

Empty Arms

Written by Stevie Ray Vaughan

Tune down 1/2 step:
(low to high) E♭-A♭-D♭-G♭

Intro-Guitar Solo
Moderately fast Blues ♩ = 152

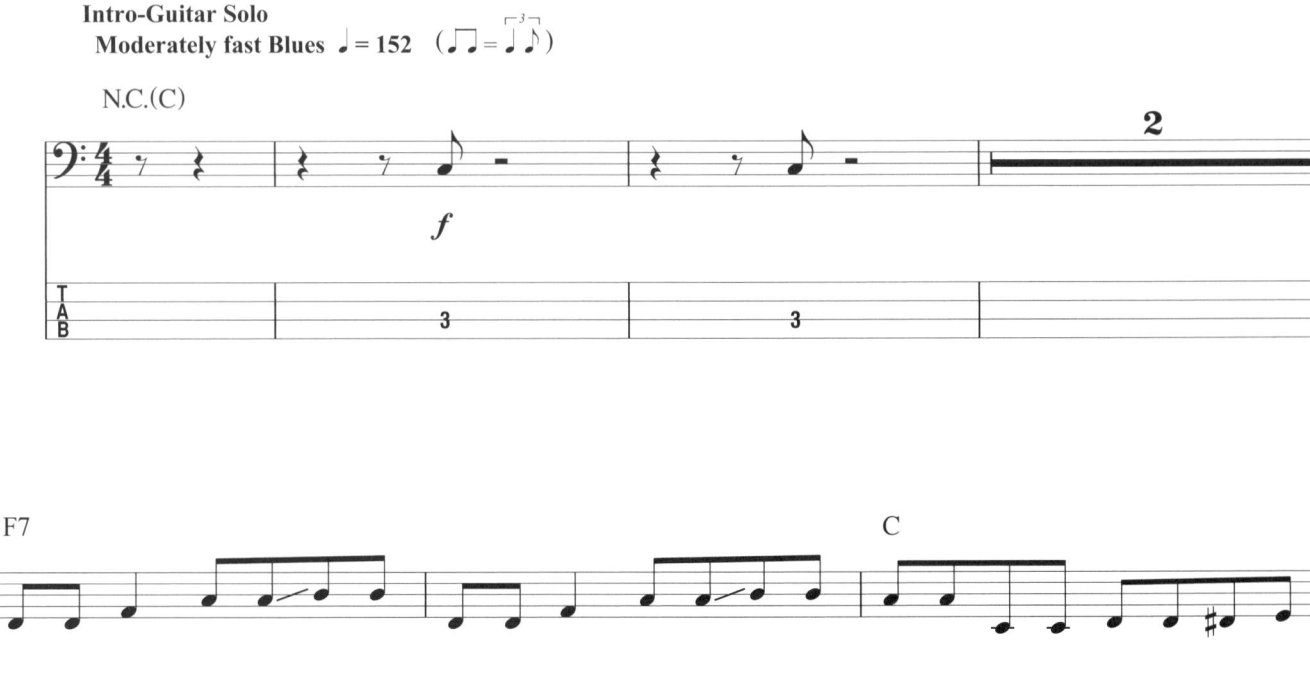

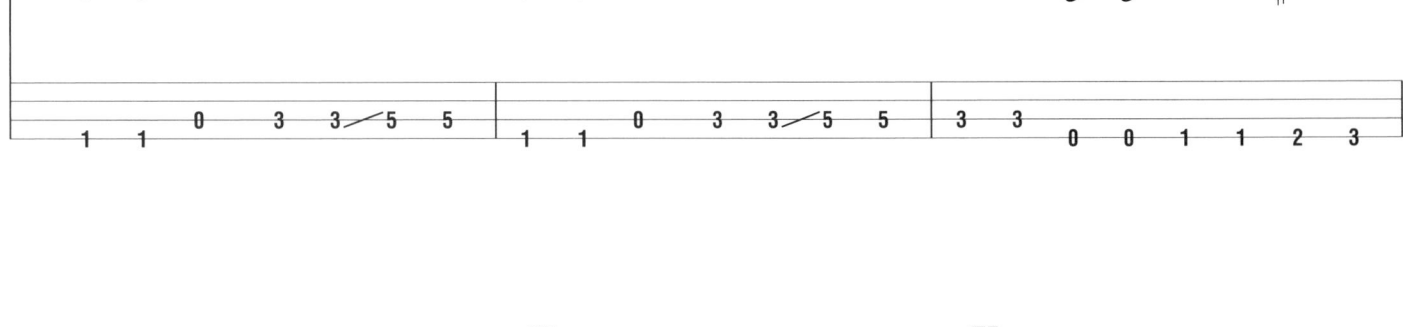

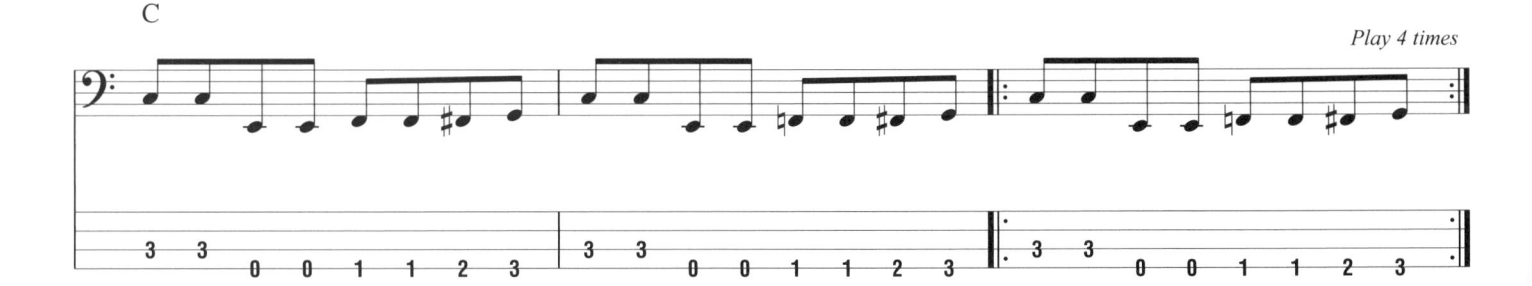

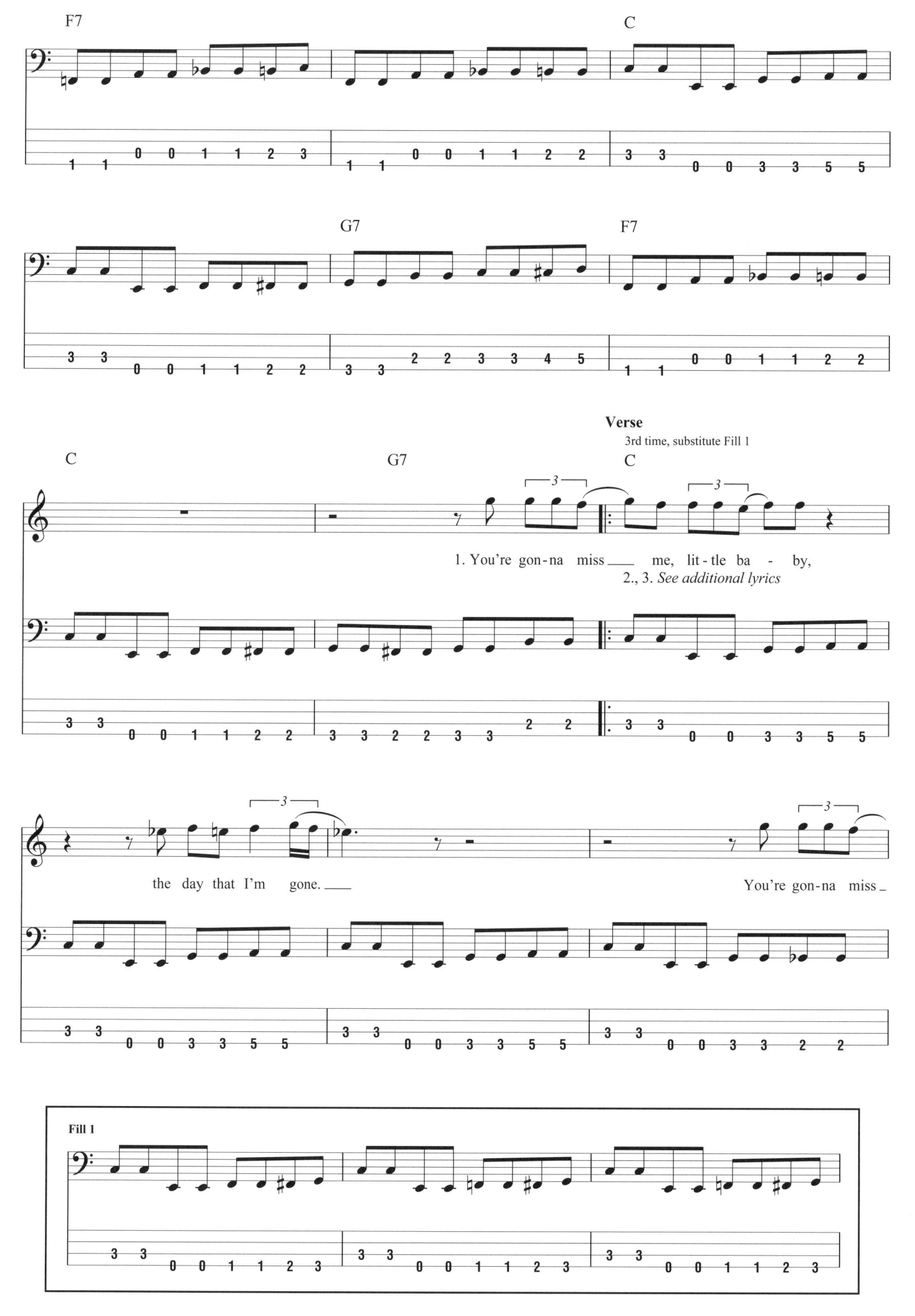

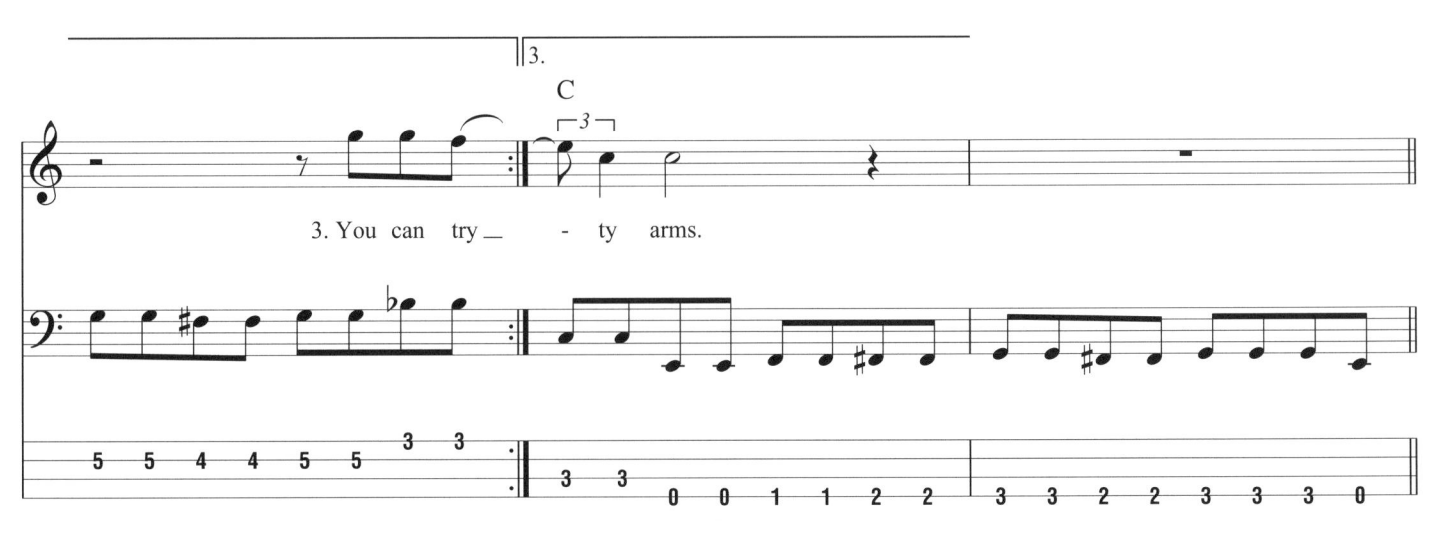

Guitar Solo

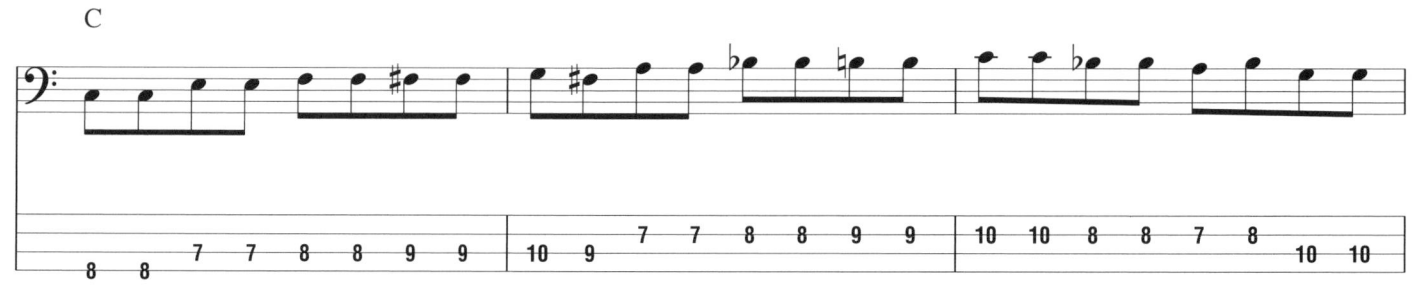

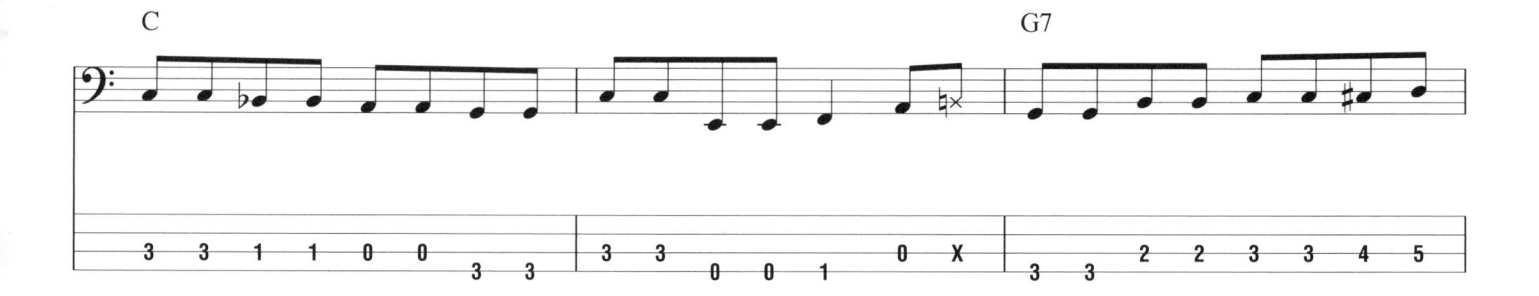

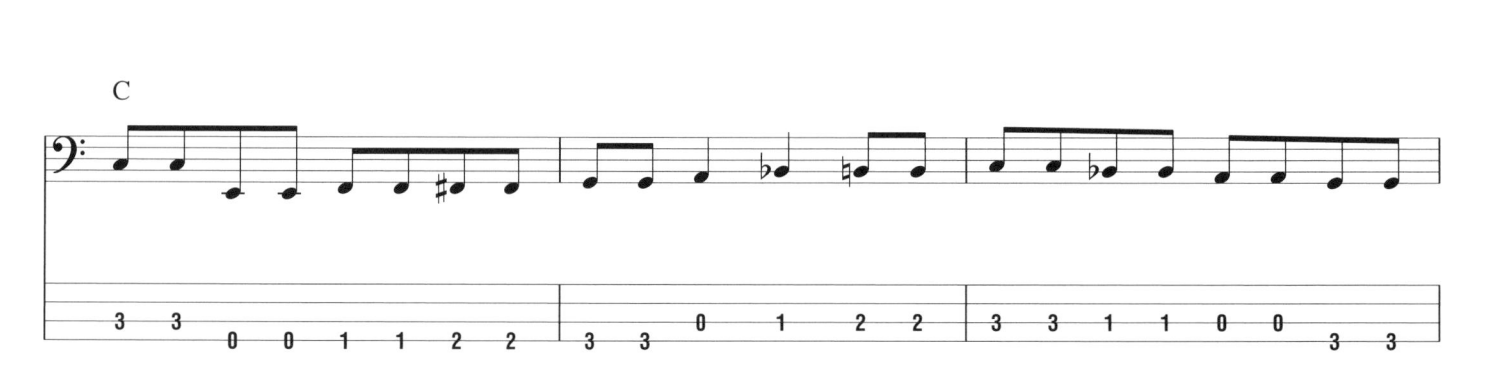

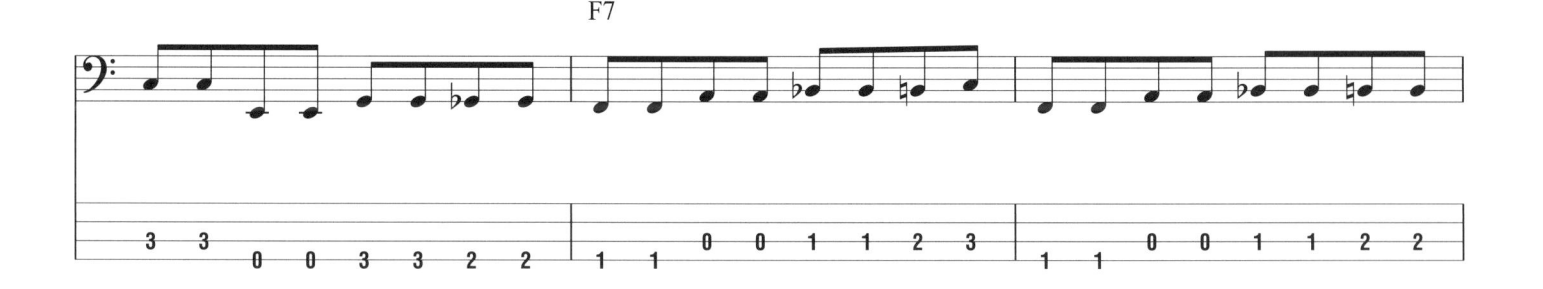

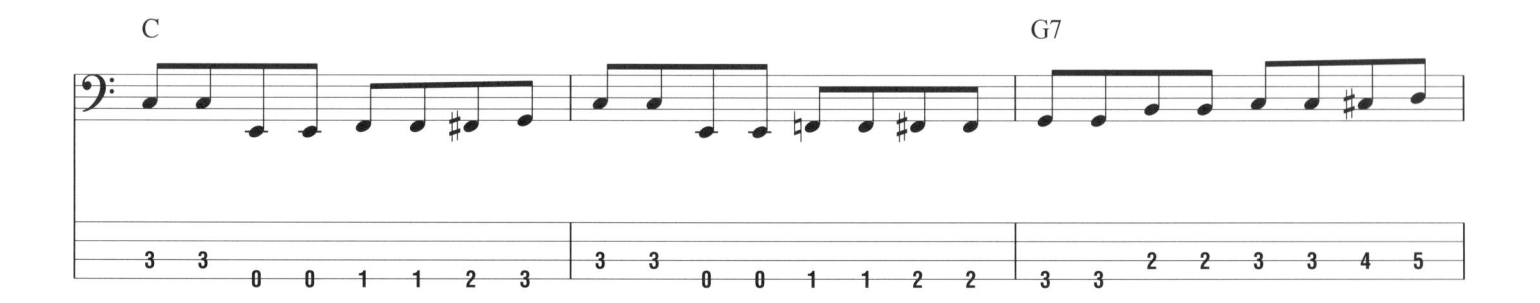

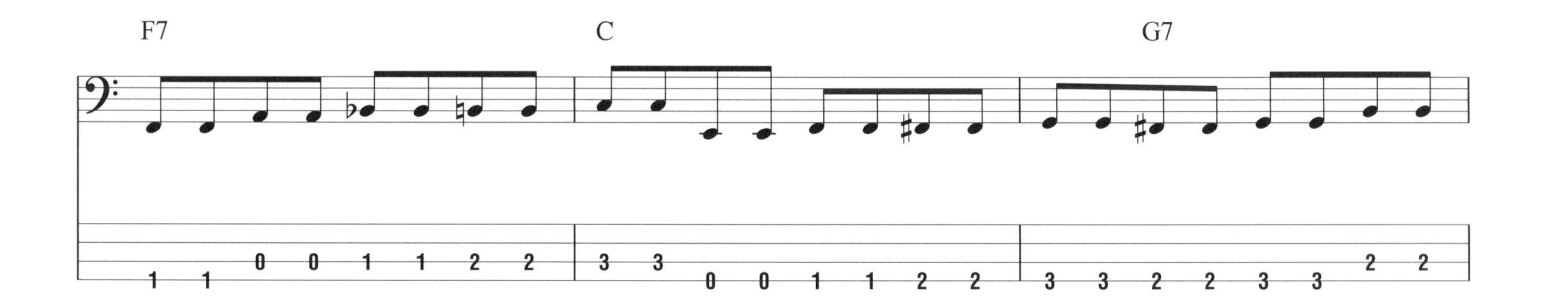

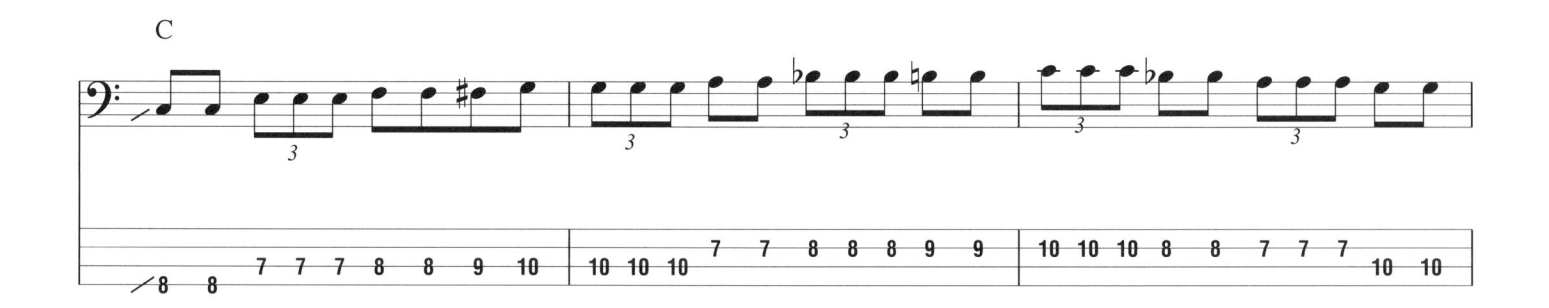

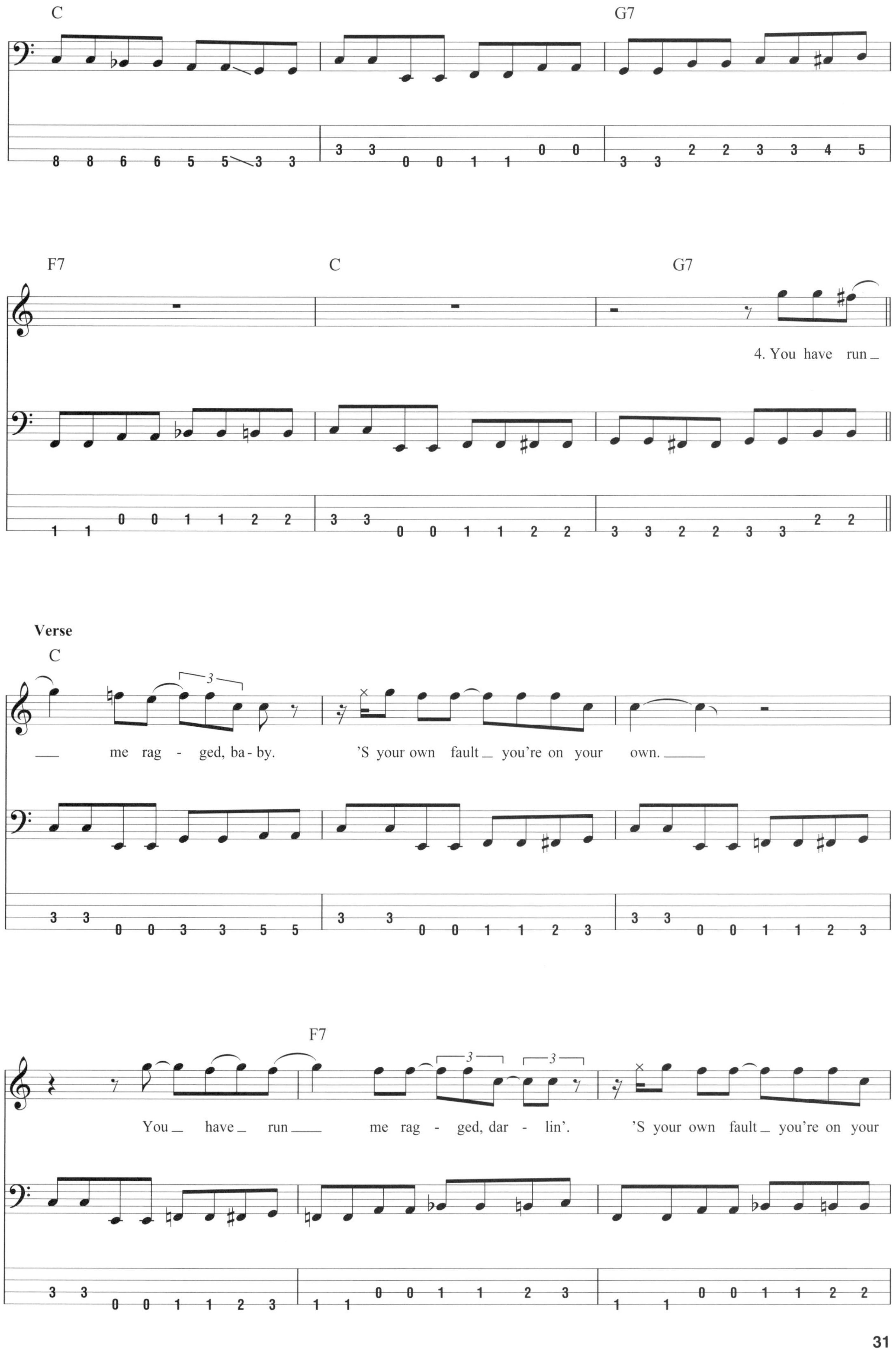

Verse

4. You have run me rag - ged, ba - by. 'S your own fault_ you're on your own._____

You_ have_ run_____ me rag - ged, dar - lin'. 'S your own fault_ you're on your

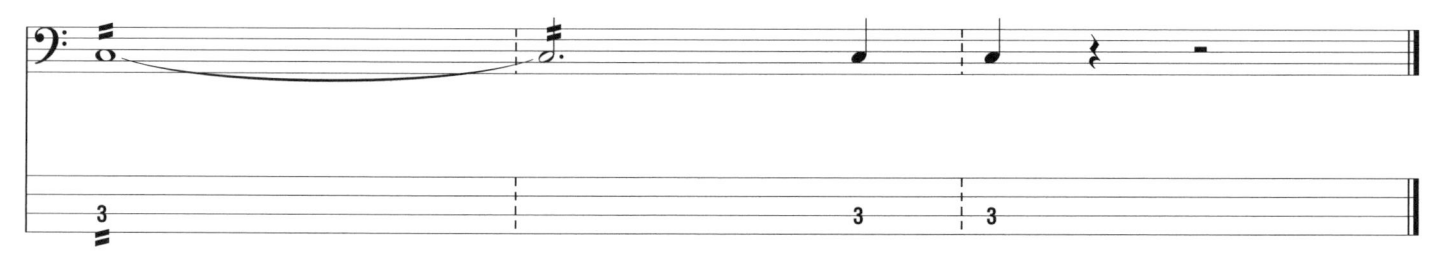

Free time

Additional Lyrics

2. You have run me ragged, baby.
   'S your own fault you're on your own.
   You have run me ragged, darlin'.
   'S your own fault you're on your own.
   You didn't want me to wait, baby,
   Till your other man was gone.

3. You can try to get me back, baby,
   With all your tricks and charms.
   You can try to get me back, baby,
   With all your tricks and charms.
   But when all your games are over,
   You'll be left with empty arms.

The House Is Rockin'

Written by Stevie Ray Vaughan and Doyle Bramhall

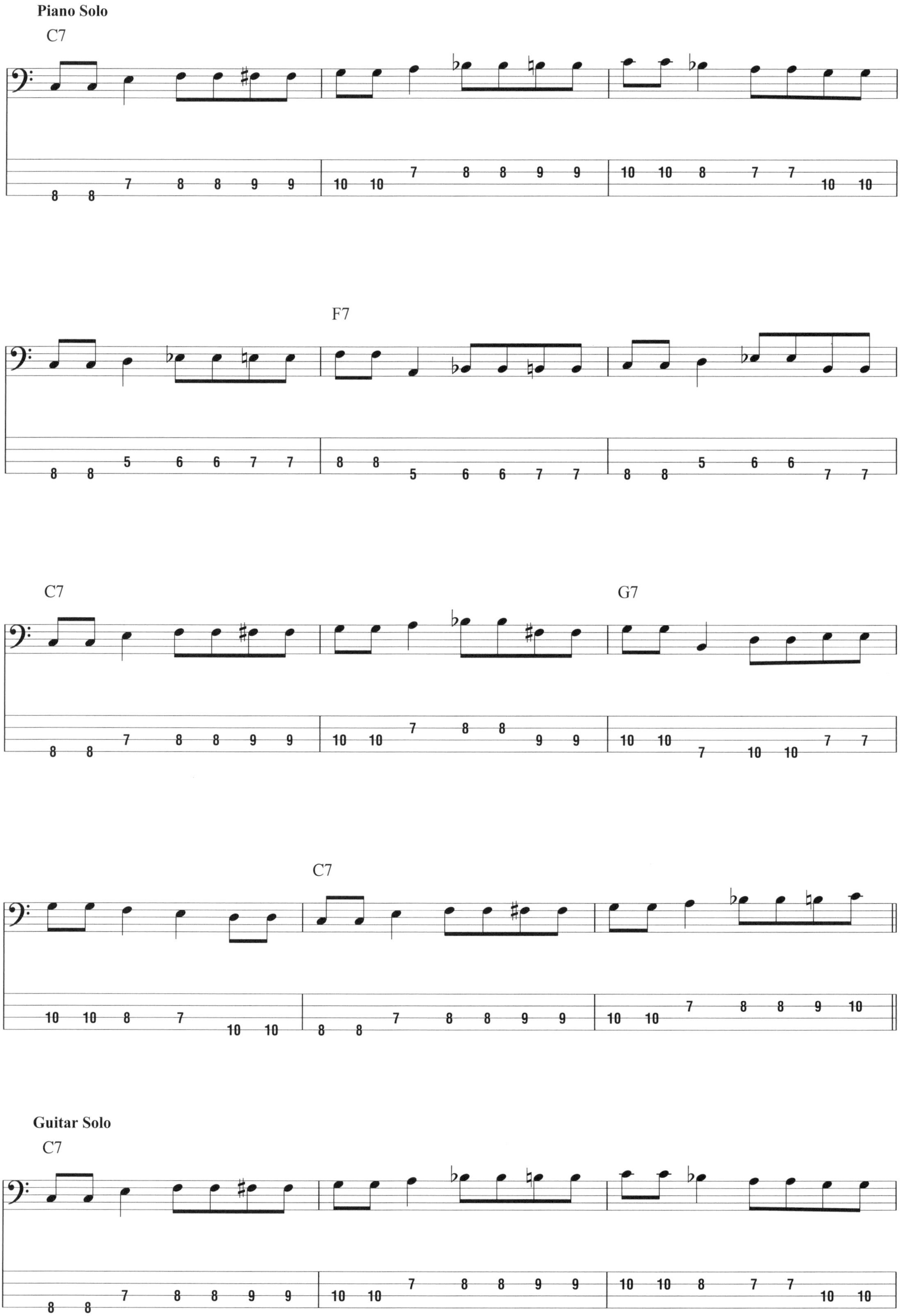
Piano Solo
C7
F7
C7
G7
C7
Guitar Solo
C7

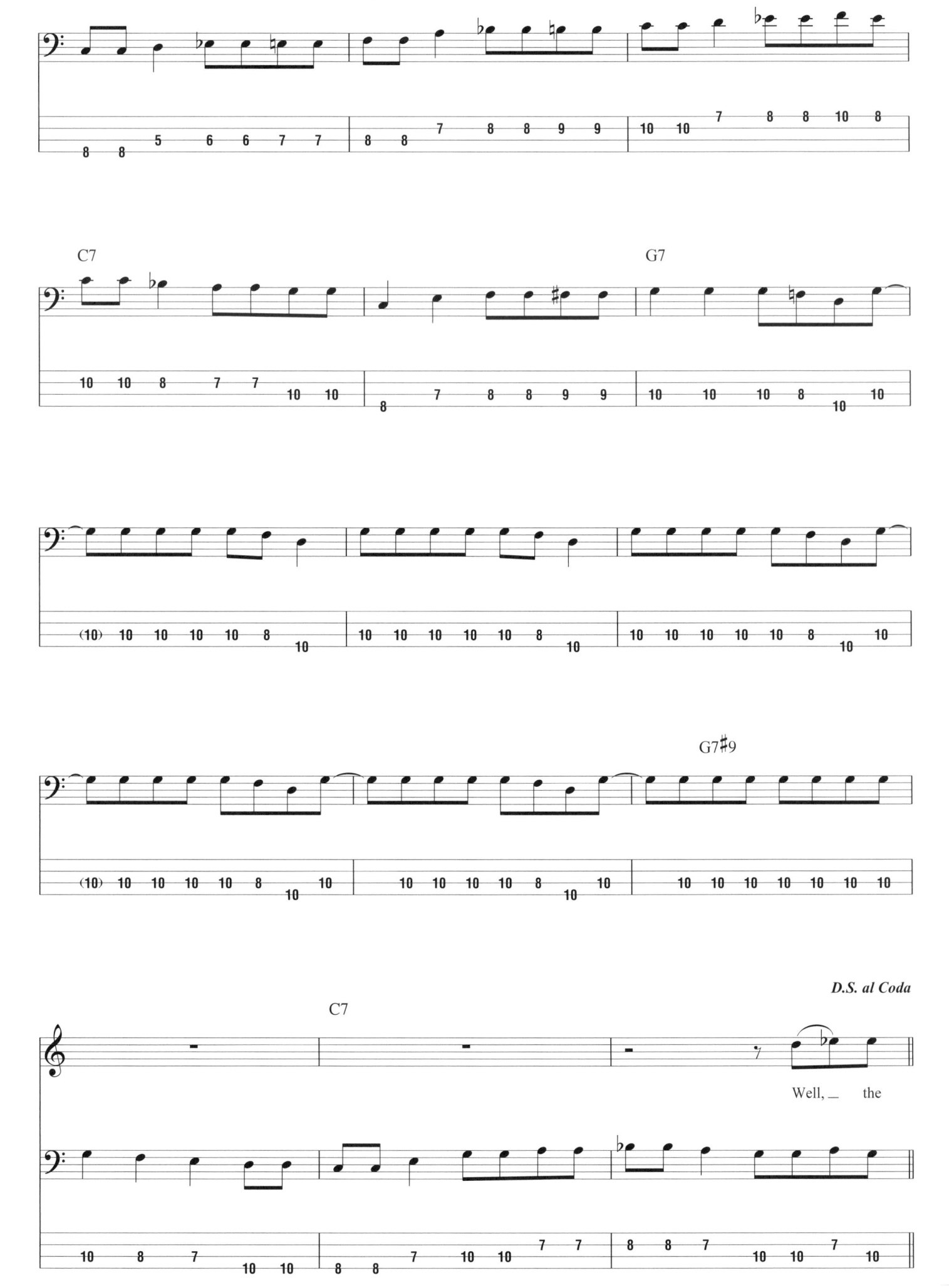

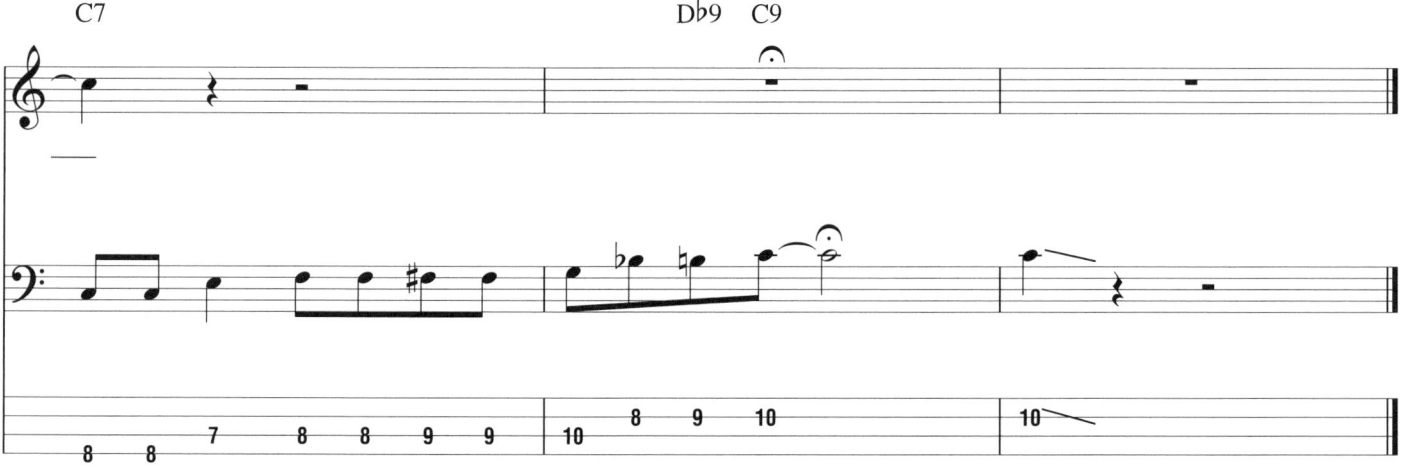

Additional Lyrics

2. Walkin' up the street, you can hear the sound
   Of some bad honky tonkers really layin' it down.
   They've seen it all for years, they got nothin' to lose.
   So get out on the floor, shimmy till you shake somethin' loose!

Love Struck Baby

Written by Stevie Ray Vaughan

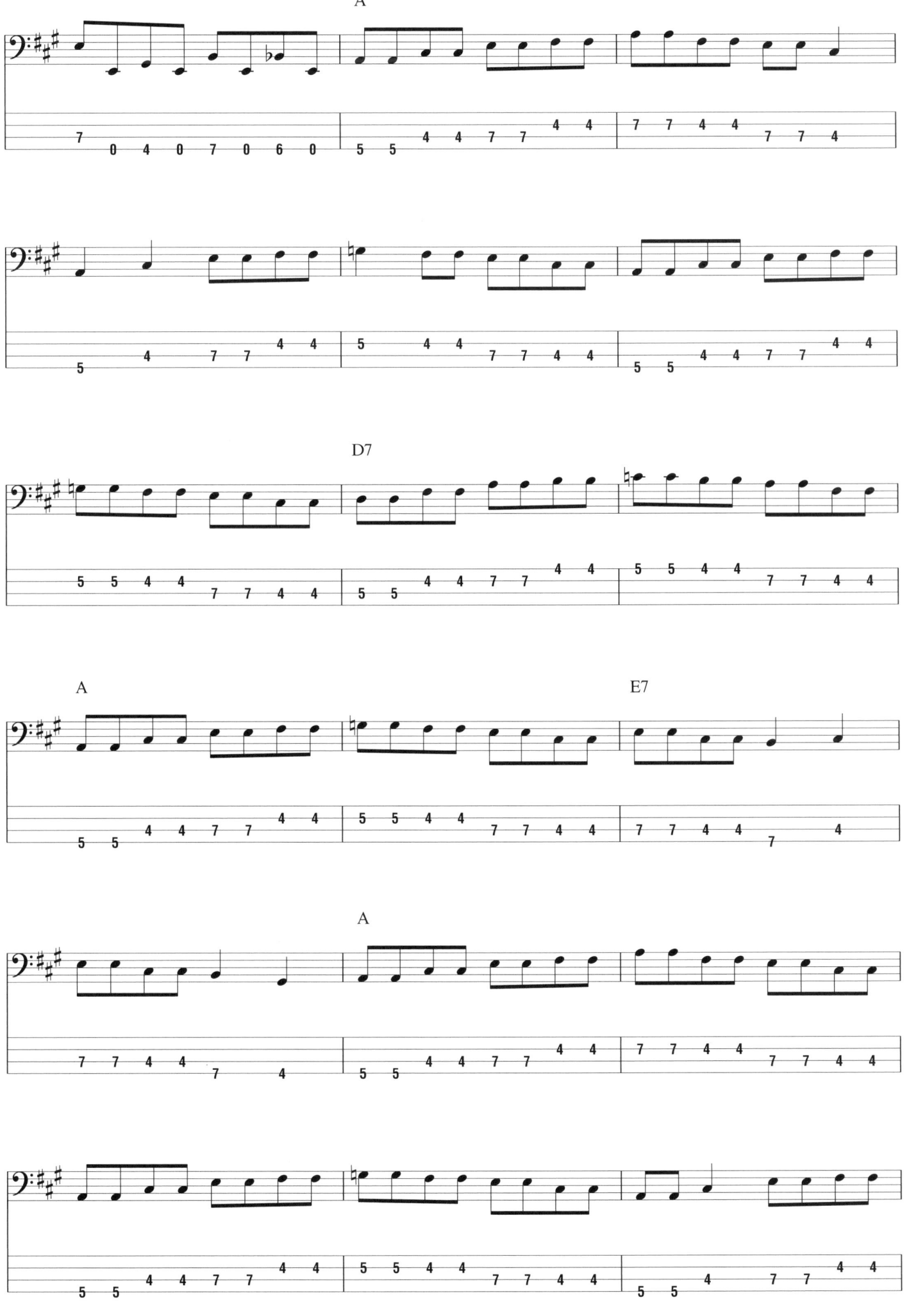

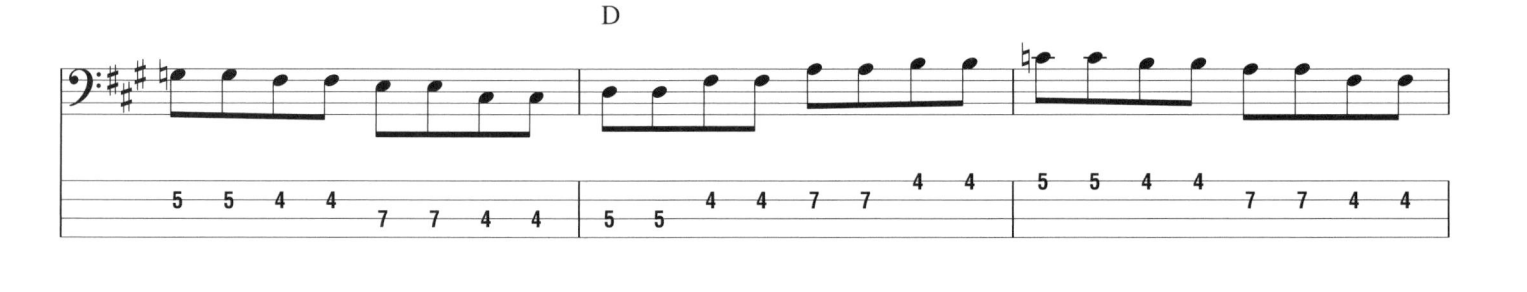

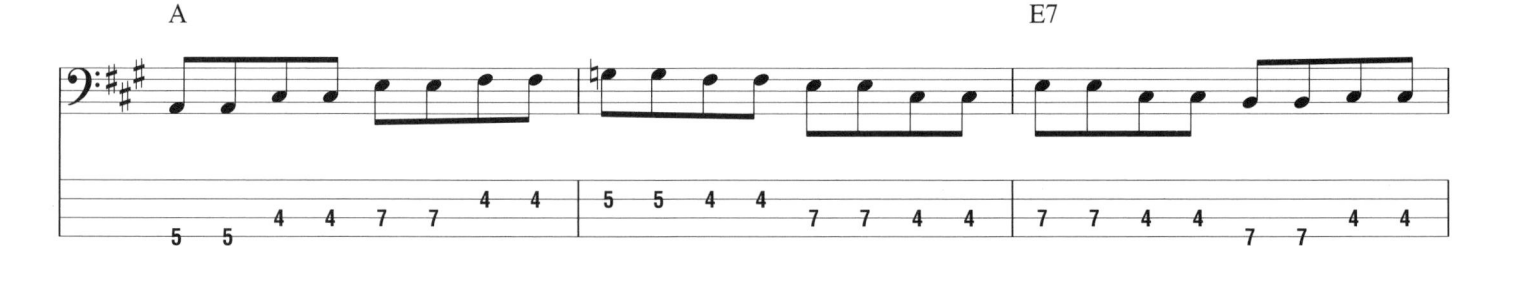

D.S. al Coda

Additional Lyrics

Pre-Chorus Sparks start flyin' ev'ry time we meet.
Let me tell you baby, you knock me off my feet.
Your kisses trip me up, they're so doggone sweet.
Don't ya know baby, you can't be beat?

The Sky Is Crying

Words and Music by Elmore James

Tune down 1/2 step:
(low to high) E♭-A♭-D♭-G♭

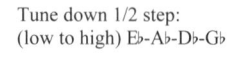

Verse
Slow Blues ♩. = 55

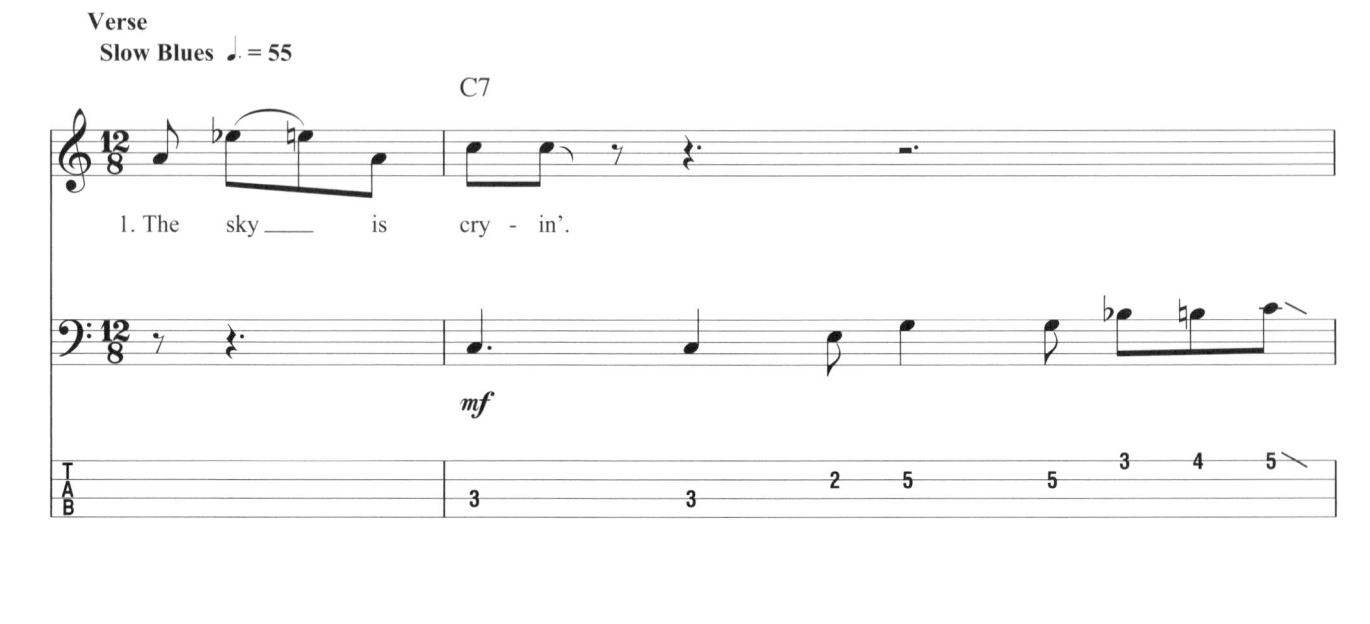

1. The sky ___ is cry - in'.

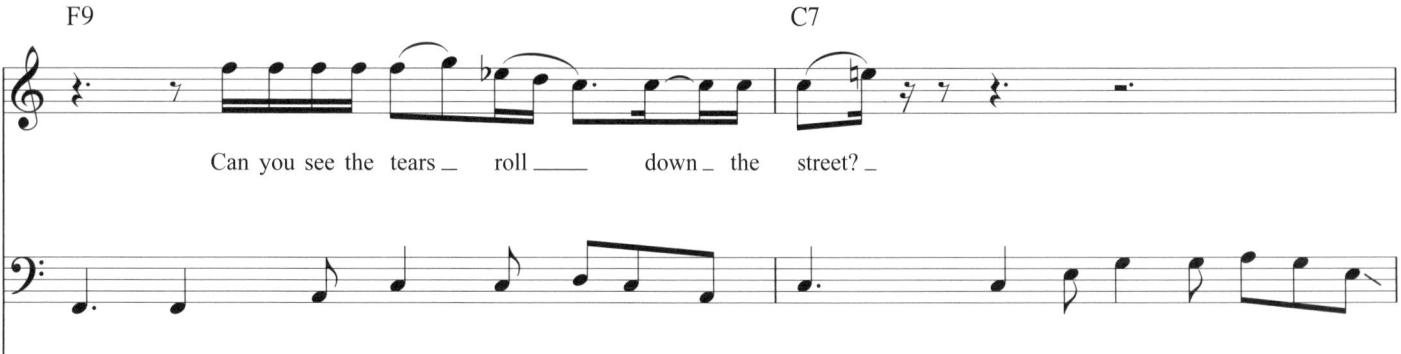

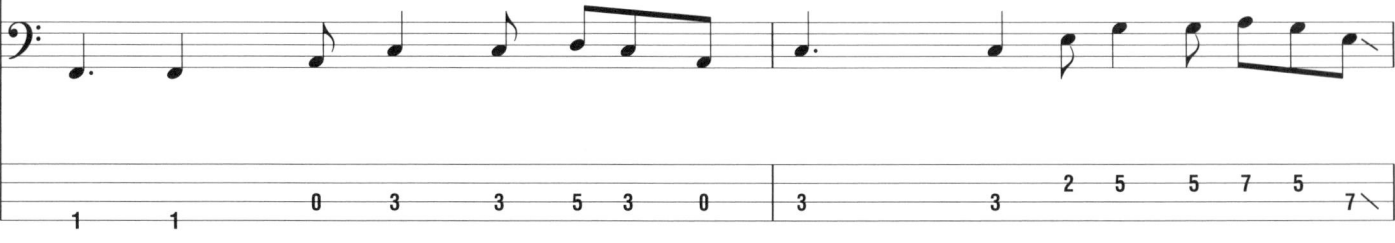

Can you see the tears ___ roll ___ down ___ the street? ___

The sky ___ is cry - in'.

made my poor heart, uh, skip a beat. ___

Guitar Solo

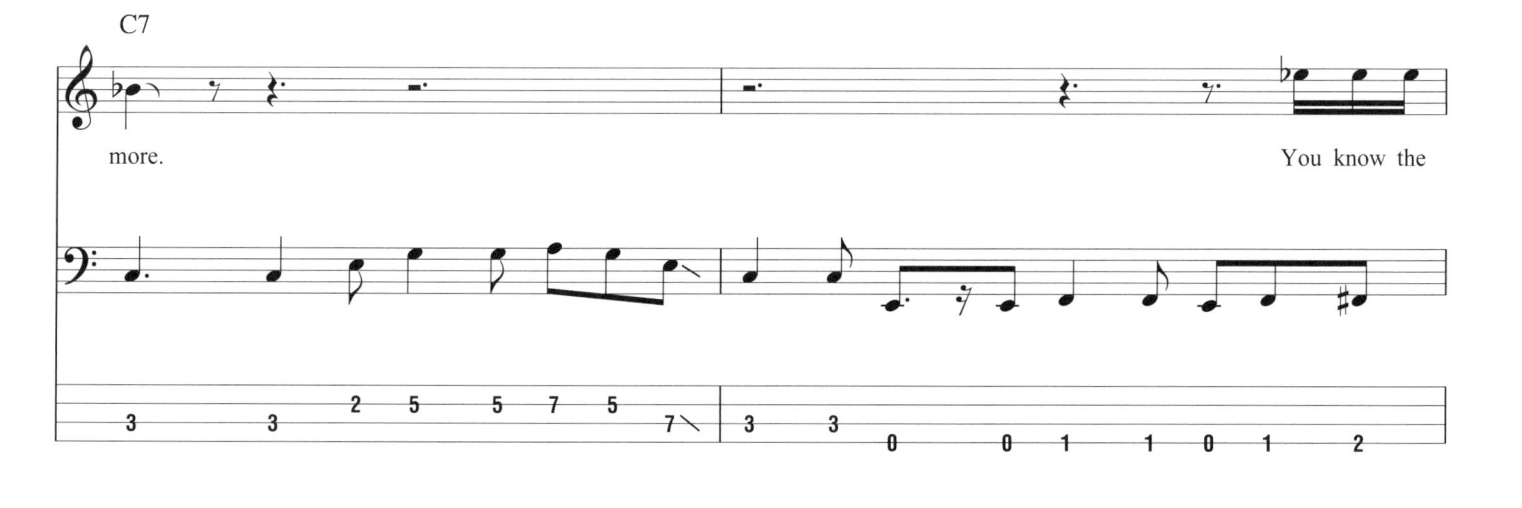

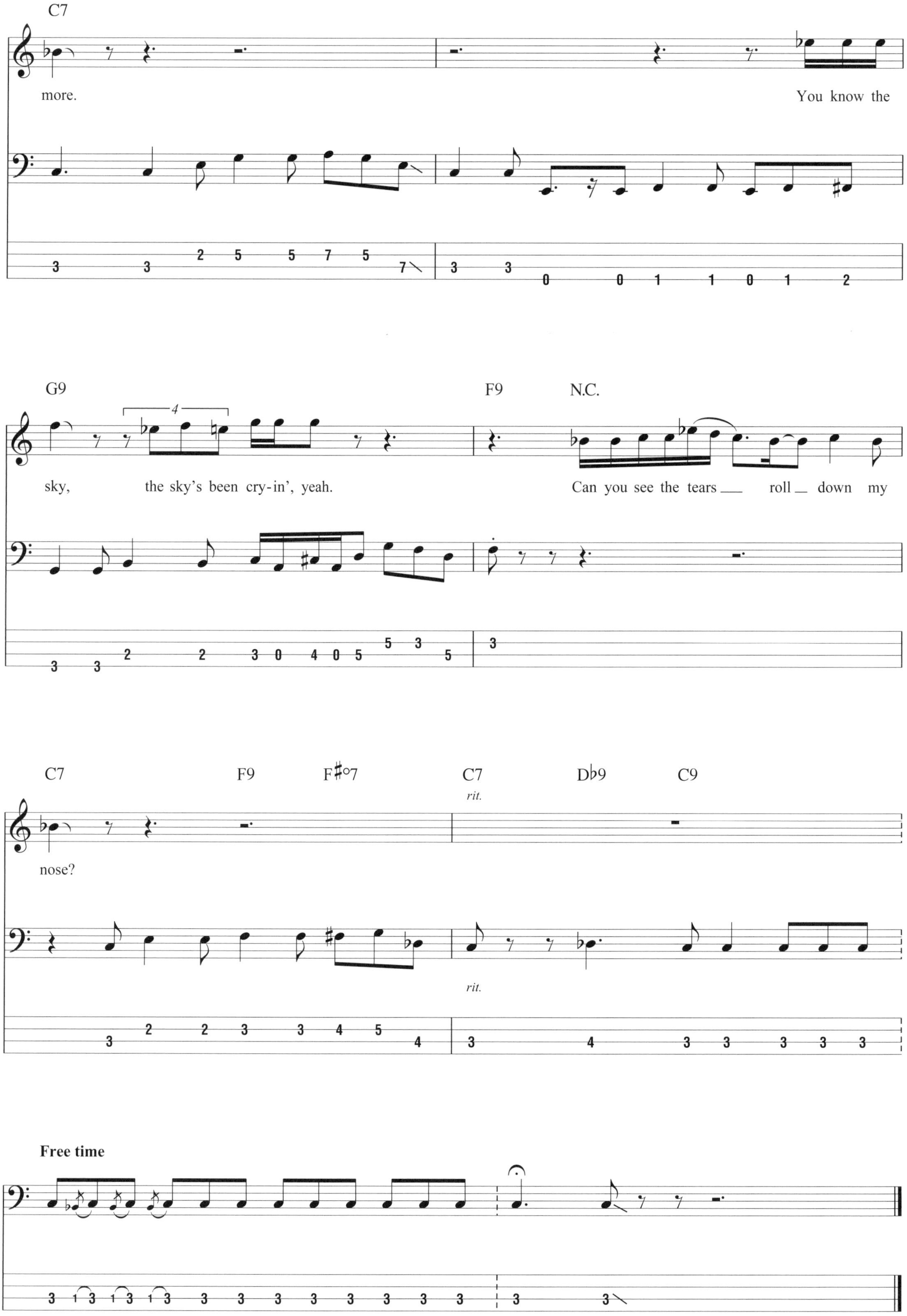

more.

You know the

sky,   the sky's been cry-in', yeah.   Can you see the tears ___ roll ___ down my

nose?

Free time

Tightrope

Written by Stevie Ray Vaughan and Doyle Bramhall

Tune down 1/2 step:
(low to high) E♭-A♭-D♭-G♭

Intro
Moderately ♩ = 98

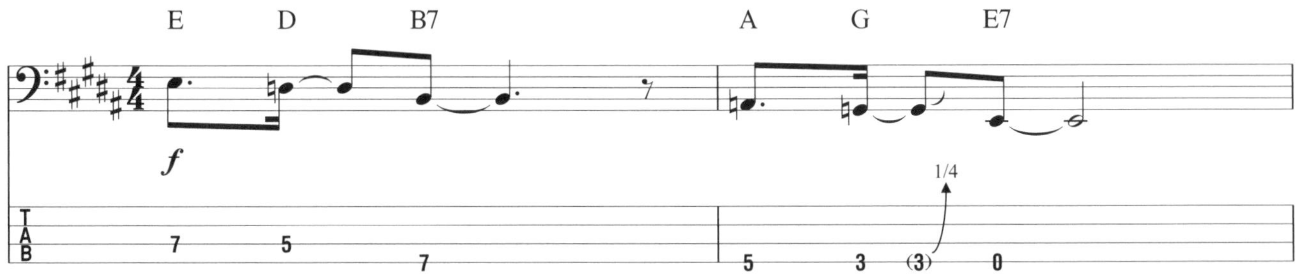

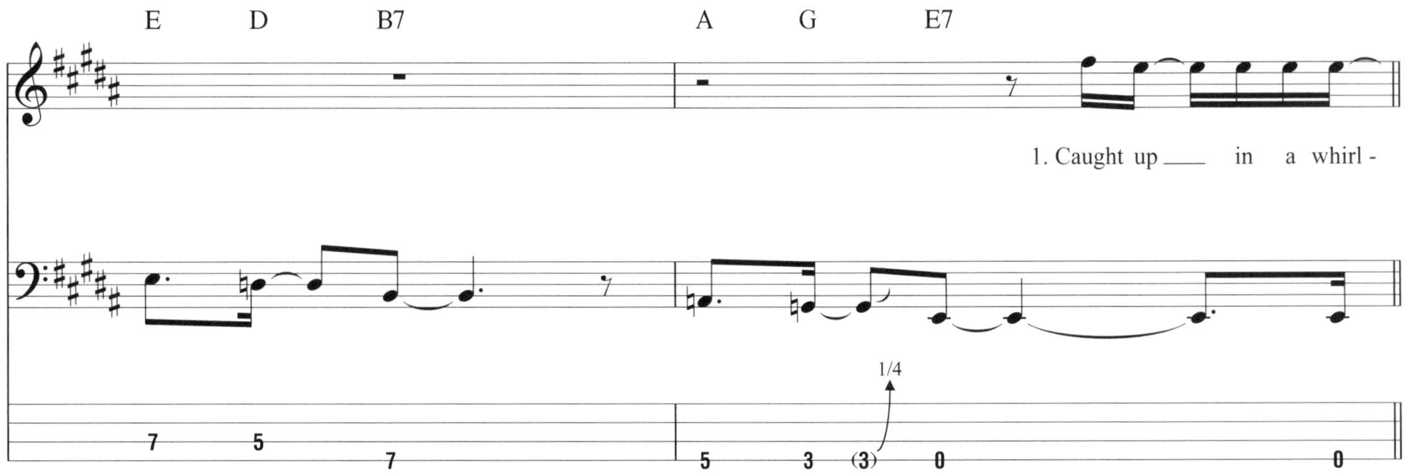

Lyrics under notation:

1. Caught up ___ in a whirl-

- wind, ___ can't catch my breath. ___ Knee-deep ___ in hot

Verse

B9

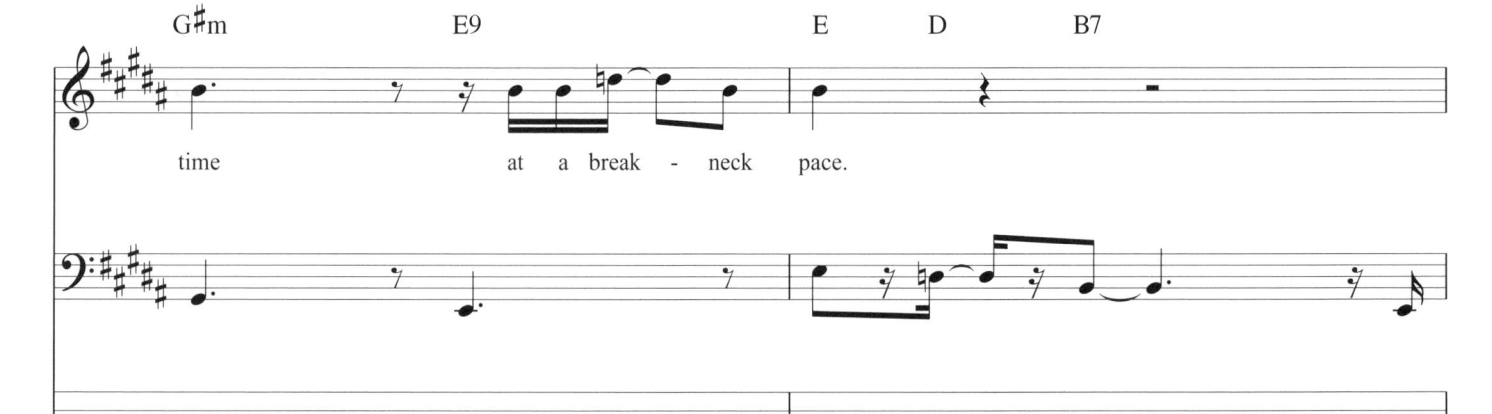

wa - ter,   broke out __ in a cold sweat.   Can't __ catch a

tur - tle   in this __ rat race.   Feels like __ I'm los - in'

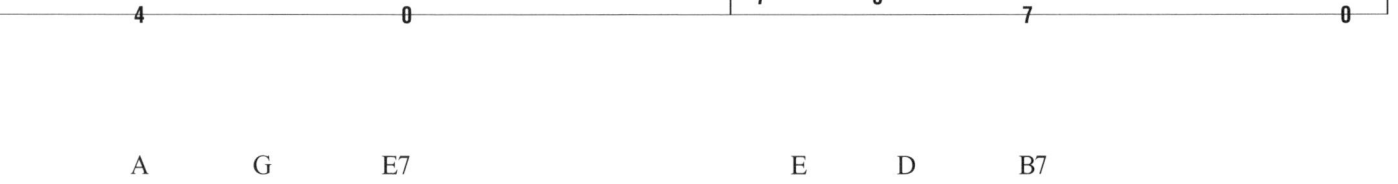

G#m   E9   E   D   B7

time   at a break - neck pace.

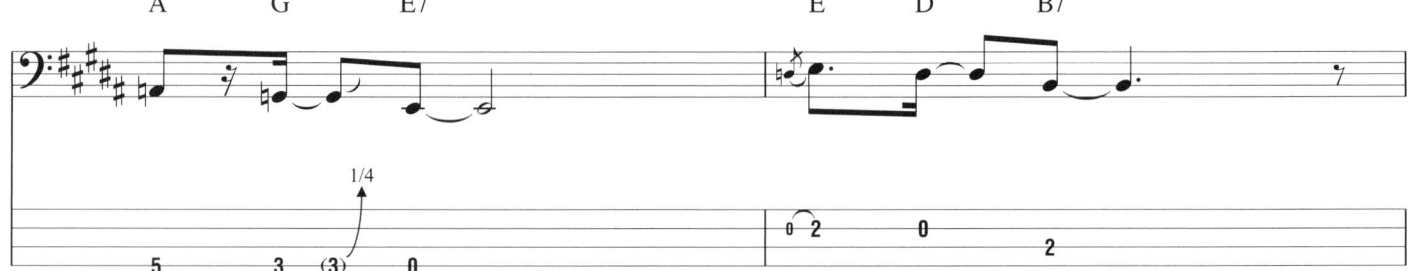

A   G   E7   E   D   B7

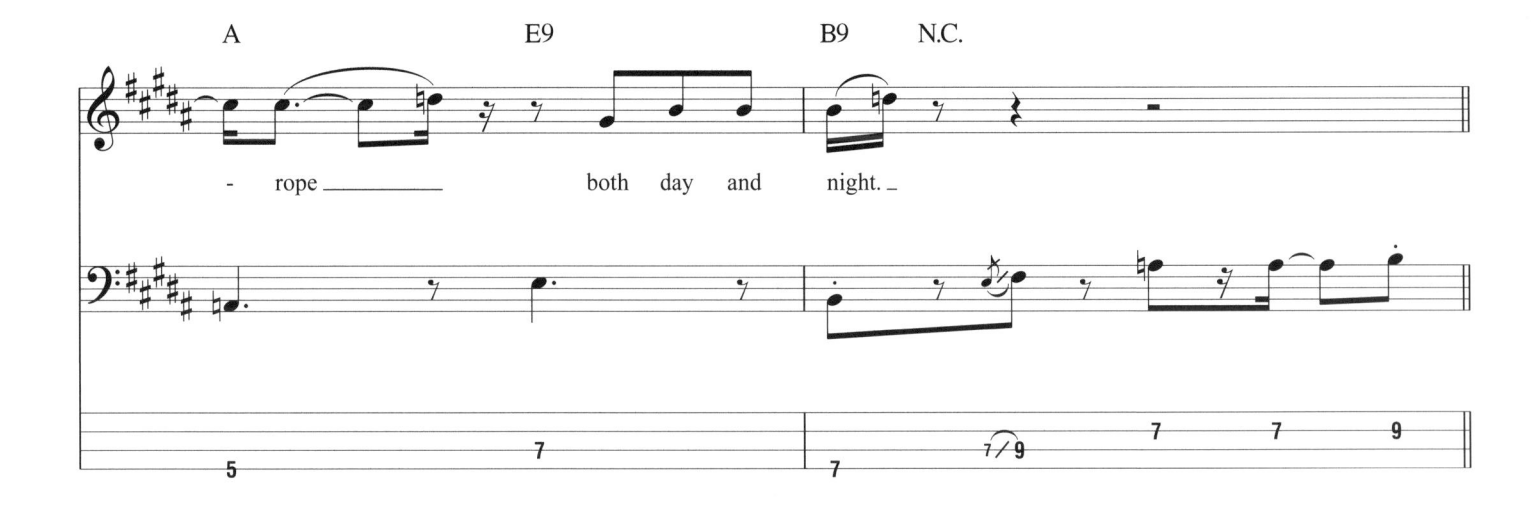

rope _____ both day and night. _

Guitar Solo

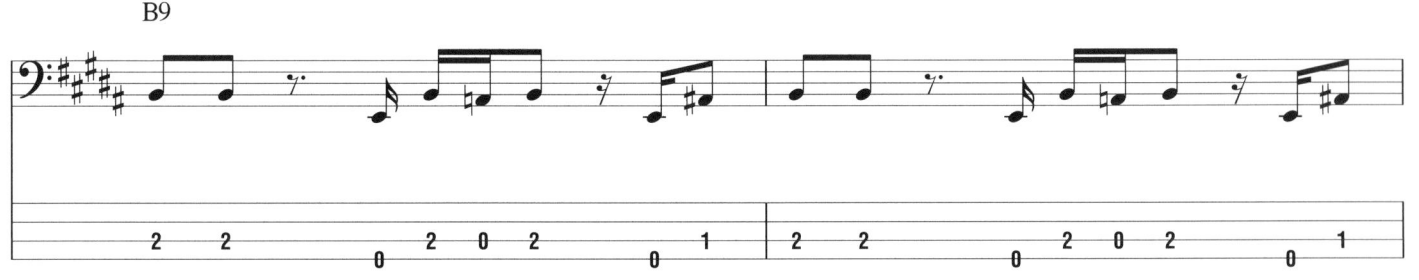

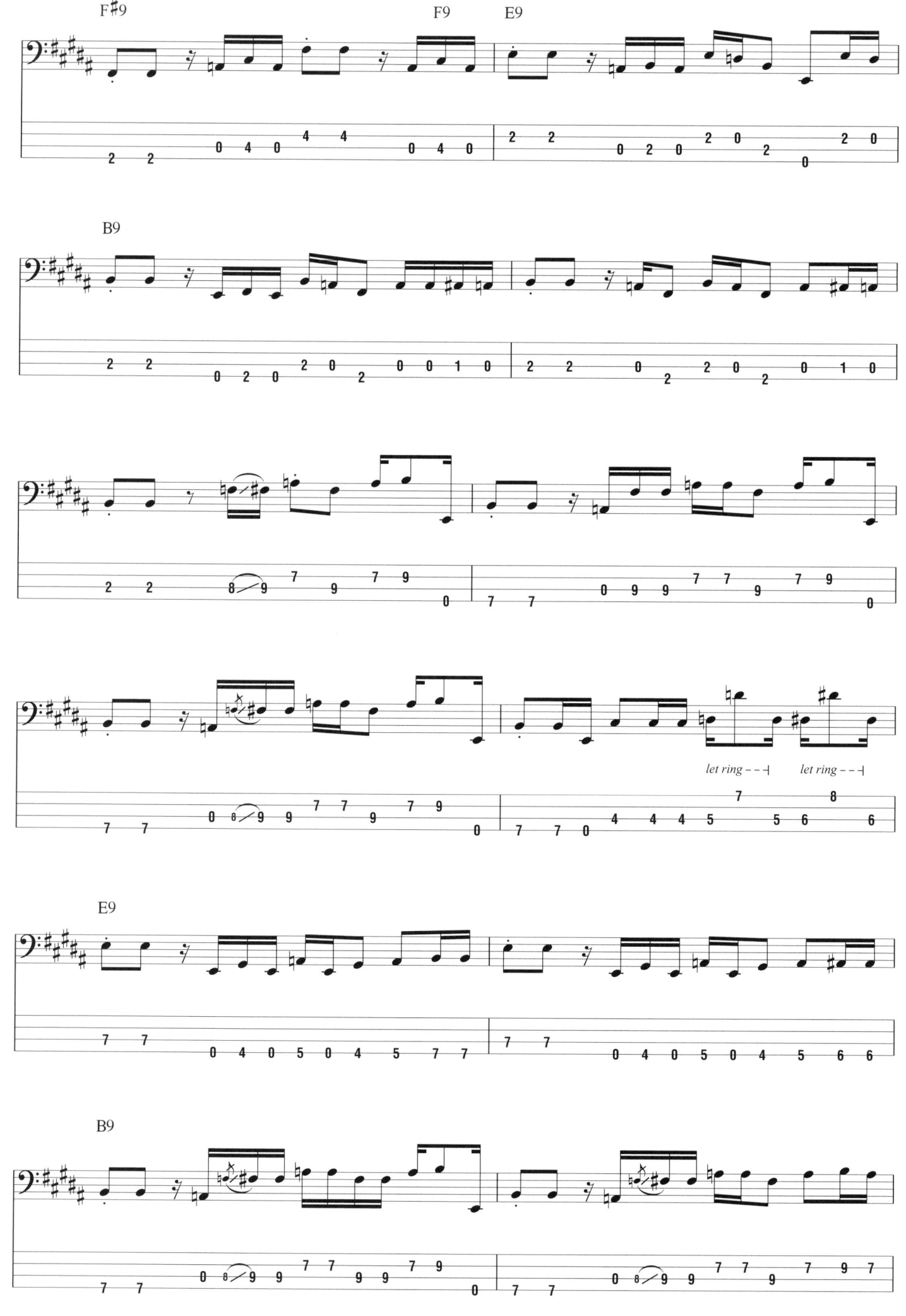

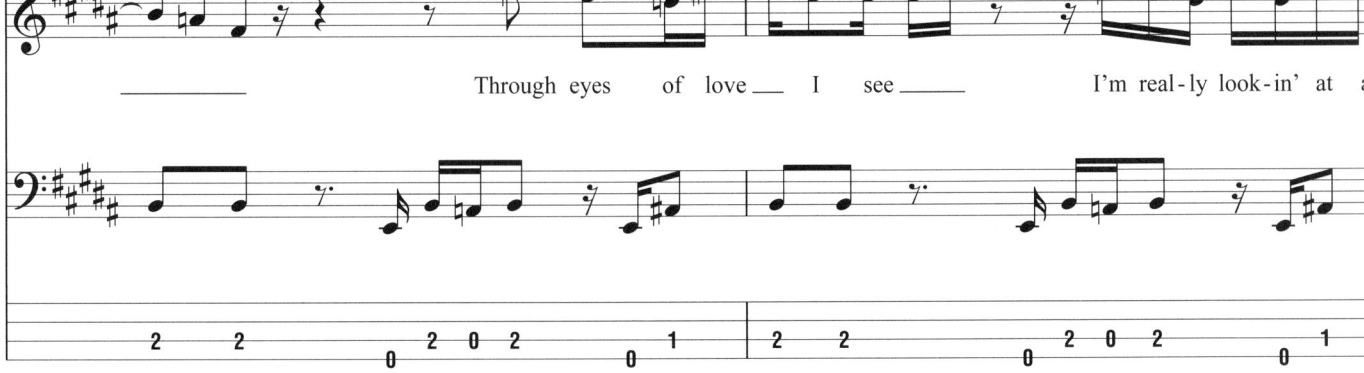

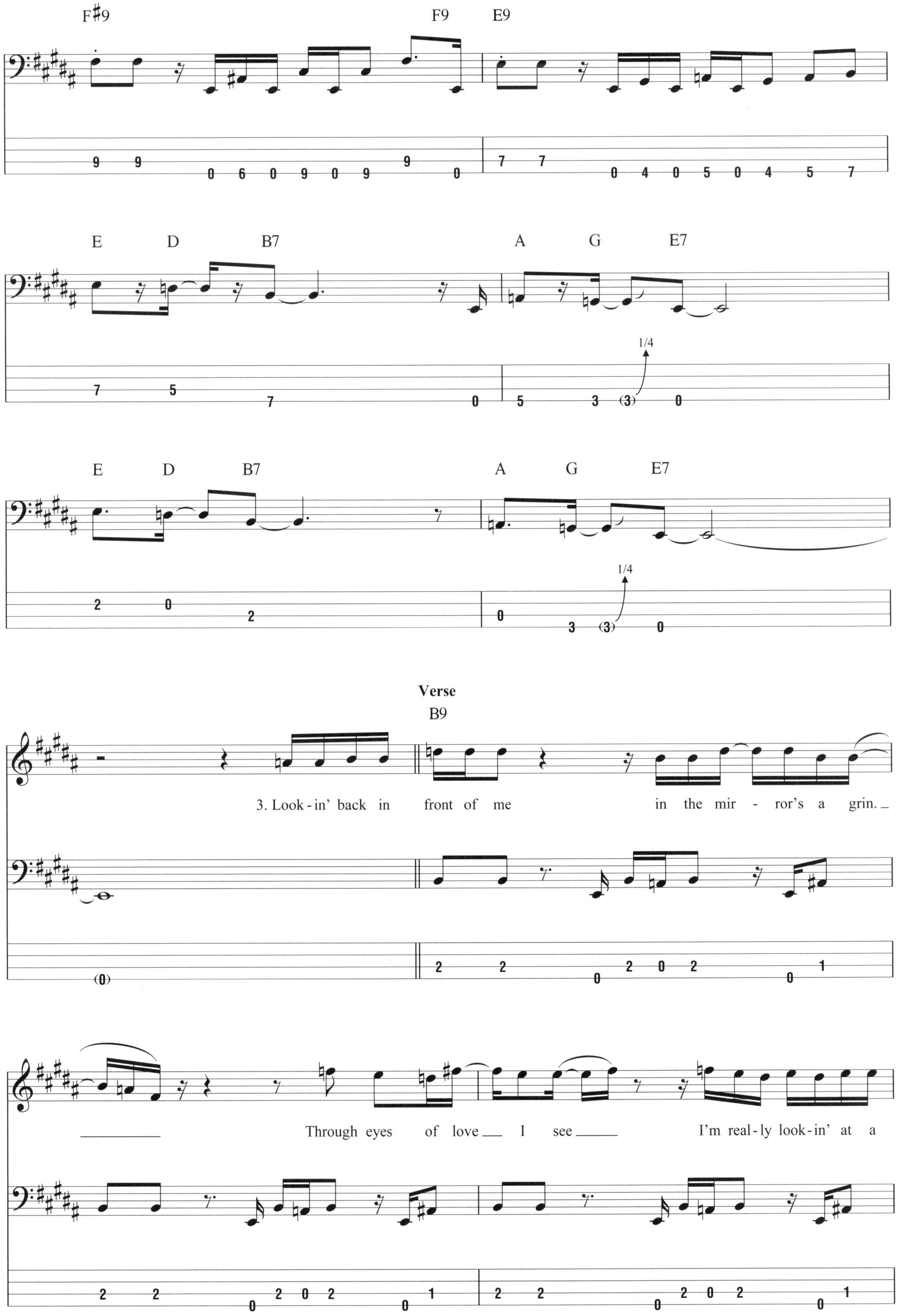
F♯9
F9
E9
E
D
B7
A
G
E7
1/4
E
D
B7
A
G
E7
1/4
Verse
B9
3. Look-in' back in front of me in the mir - ror's a grin.
Through eyes of love I see
I'm real-ly look-in' at a

Outro-Guitar Solo

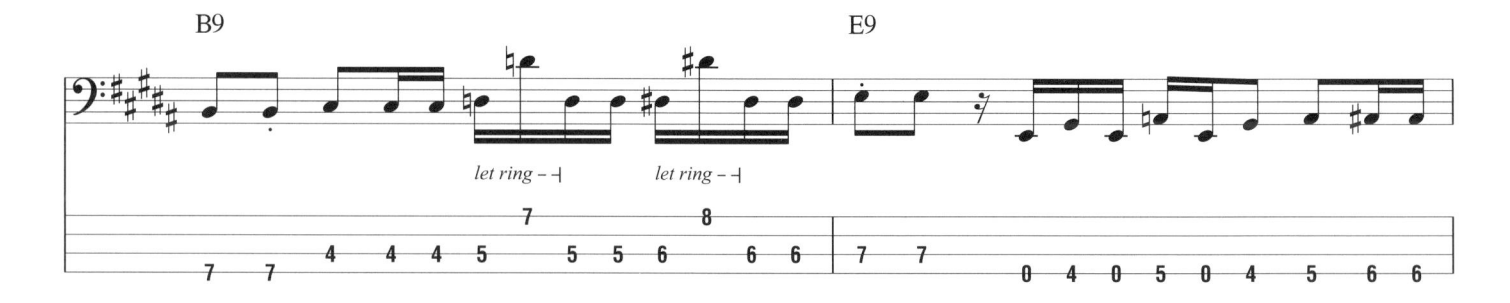

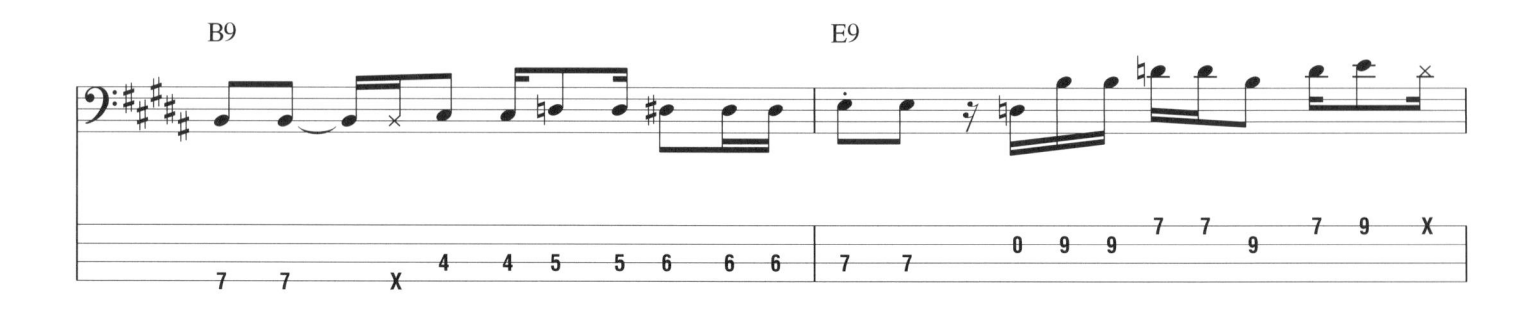

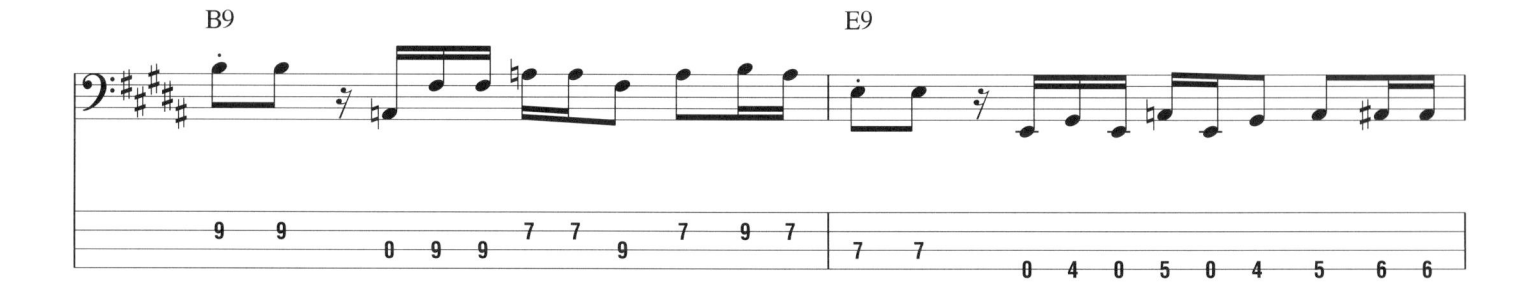

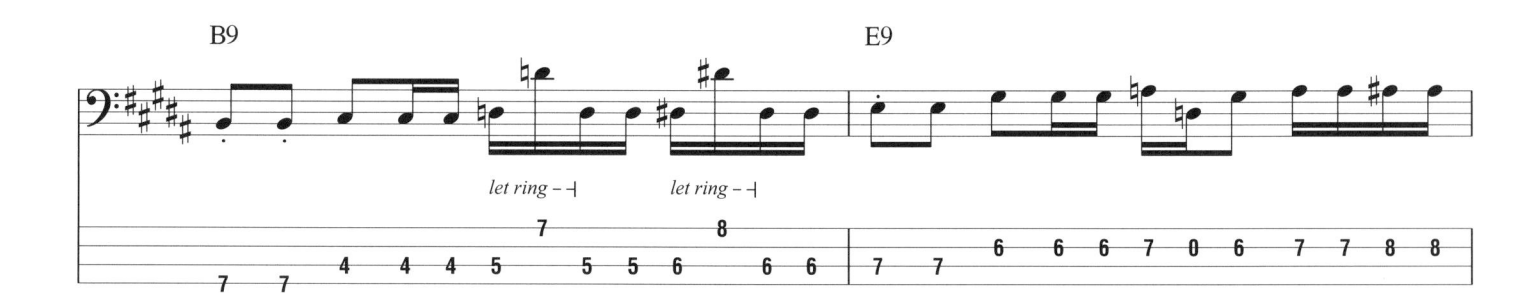

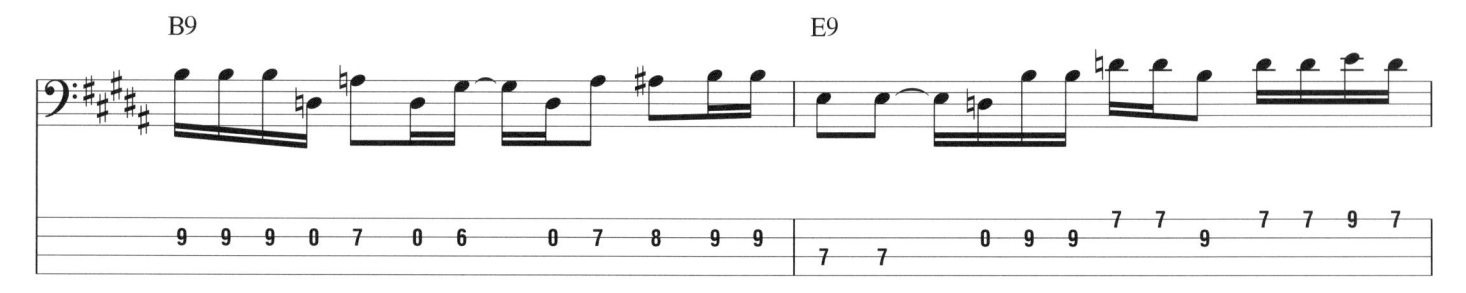

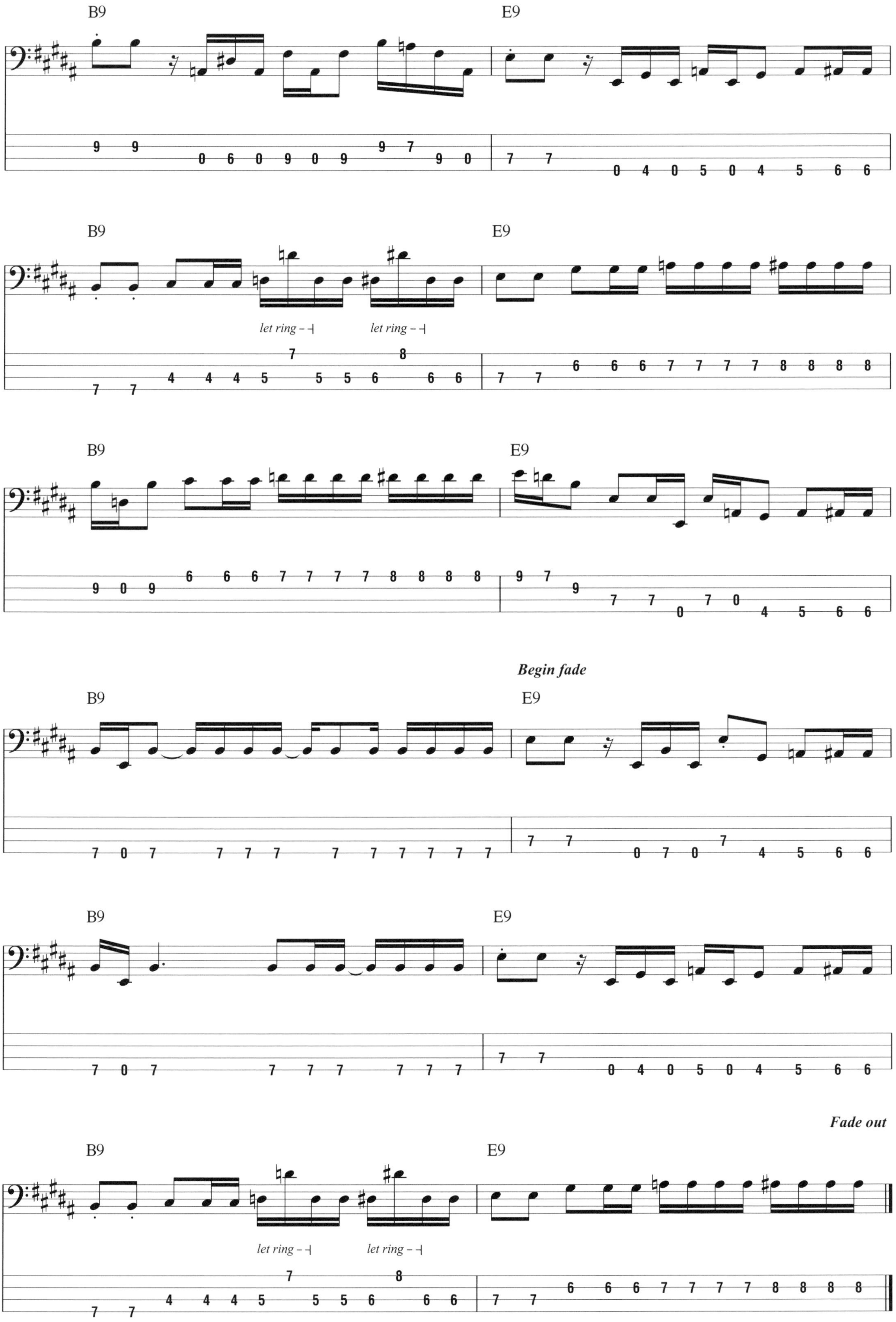
B9
E9
B9
E9
let ring
let ring
B9
E9
Begin fade
B9
E9
B9
E9
Fade out
B9
E9
let ring
let ring

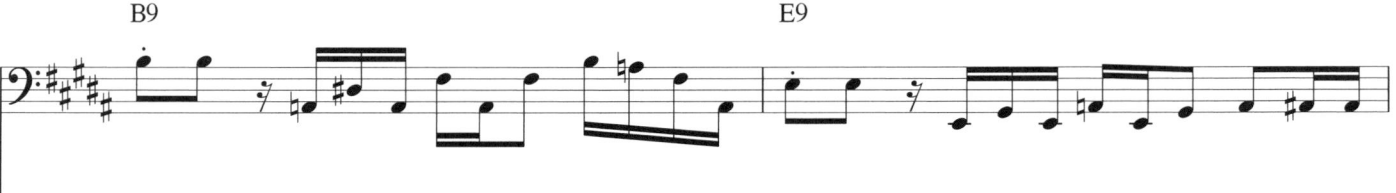

BASS NOTATION LEGEND

Bass music can be notated two different ways: on a *musical staff,* and in *tablature*

Notes:

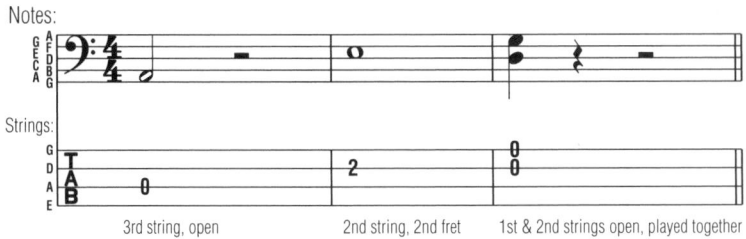

THE MUSICAL STAFF shows pitches and rhythms and is divided by bar lines into measures. Pitches are named after the first seven letters of the alphabet.

TABLATURE graphically represents the bass fingerboard. Each horizontal line represents a string, and each number represents a fret.

3rd string, open   2nd string, 2nd fret   1st & 2nd strings open, played together

---

HAMMER-ON: Strike the first (lower) note with one finger, then sound the higher note (on the same string) with another finger by fretting it without picking.

PULL-OFF: Place both fingers on the notes to be sounded. Strike the first note and without picking, pull the finger off to sound the second (lower) note.

LEGATO SLIDE: Strike the first note and then slide the same fret-hand finger up or down to the second note. The second note is not struck.

SHIFT SLIDE: Same as legato slide, except the second note is struck.

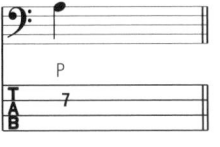

TRILL: Very rapidly alternate between the notes indicated by continuously hammering on and pulling off.

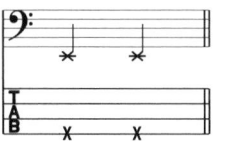

TREMOLO PICKING: The note is picked as rapidly and continuously as possible.

VIBRATO: The string is vibrated by rapidly bending and releasing the note with the fretting hand.

SHAKE: Using one finger, rapidly alternate between two notes on one string by sliding either a half-step above or below.

NATURAL HARMONIC: Strike the note while the fret hand lightly touches the string directly over the fret indicated.

Harm.

MUFFLED STRINGS: A percussive sound is produced by laying the fret hand across the string(s) without depressing them and striking them with the pick hand.

BEND: Strike the note and bend up the interval shown.

1/2

BEND AND RELEASE: Strike the note and bend up as indicated, then release back to the original note. Only the first note is struck.

1/2

RIGHT-HAND TAP: Hammer ("tap") the fret indicated with the "pick-hand" index or middle finger and pull off to the note fretted by the fret hand.

+

LEFT-HAND TAP: Hammer ("tap") the fret indicated with the "fret-hand" index or middle finger.

⊕

SLAP: Strike ("slap") string with right-hand thumb.

T

POP: Snap ("pop") string with right-hand index or middle finger.

P

Additional Musical Definitions

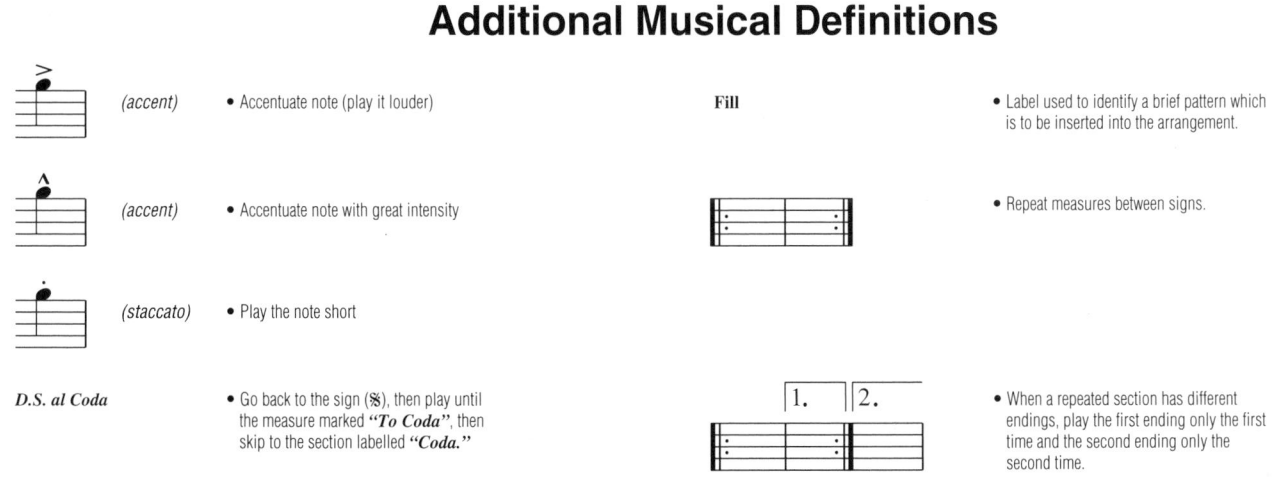

> *(accent)*	• Accentuate note (play it louder)	**Fill** • Label used to identify a brief pattern which is to be inserted into the arrangement.
^ *(accent)*	• Accentuate note with great intensity	• Repeat measures between signs.
• *(staccato)*	• Play the note short	
D.S. al Coda	• Go back to the sign (𝄋), then play until the measure marked ***"To Coda"***, then skip to the section labelled ***"Coda."***	1. 2. • When a repeated section has different endings, play the first ending only the first time and the second ending only the second time.